ACT IT OUT

ACT
IT OUT
ONE YEAR OF SOCIAL SKILLS LESSONS
FOR STUDENTS GRADES 7-12
SOUND
DATE
PROD.CO.
DIRECTOR JEANNIE STEFONEK
SOCIAL SKILLS FOR TEENS
WITH AUTISM SPECTRUM DISORDER
AND RELATED DISORDERS

AAPC
PUBLISHING

11209 Strang Line Road
Lenexa, Kansas 66215
www.aapcpublishing.net

Interior design by Stephen Tiano.

Publisher's Cataloging-In-Publication

Stefonek, Jeannie, author.
Act it out! : social skills for teens with autism spectrum disorder and related disorders / Jeannie Stefonek.
"One year of social skills lessons for students grades 7-12"--Cover. | Includes bibliographical references.

ISBN: 978-1-942197-19-5 | LCCN: 2016944671

LCSH: Social skills in adolescence--Study and teaching. | Social interaction in adolescence--Study and teaching. | Acting games--Psychological aspects--Study and teaching. | Youth with autism spectrum disorders--Behavior modification--Study and teaching. | Autistic youth--Behavior modification--Study and teaching. | Autistic youth--Education--Social aspects--Study and teaching | Teachers of children with disabilities--Handbooks, manuals, etc.

LCC: LC4717.8 .S74 2016 | DDC: 371.94--dc23

TABLE OF CONTENTS

ACKNOWLEDGMENTS

This book is a tribute to Cindy Swierenga, who co-taught the social skills group that inspired many of these pages. It also goes out my many supporters, including Mike, Sophie, and Axel Uhlenkamp; the students, parents, staff, administration, and school board at Redwood Area Schools; my editors, Kirsten McBride and Meg Utz; Jan Ellingworth; MaryAnn Roeske; Kari Dunn Buron; Camp Friendship, Redwood Falls; Grant Gronau; and Dr. Tony Attwood. Thank you everyone! Also, a special thanks goes out to the Calf Fiend Café for "my spot" to sit and work while enjoying many cups of outstanding coffee. The journey has been well worth it!

INTRODUCTION

Welcome to your new social skills curriculum! During my past fourteen years as an educator, I have learned that students greatly benefit from social skills lessons that are presented in an interesting format, with complex social behaviors broken down into concrete steps that can be practiced and generalized and therefore internalized (Krasny, Williams, Provencal, & Ozonoff, 2003).

In addition, research confirms the obvious fact that students with autism spectrum disorder (ASD) have a great deal of difficulty generalizing social skills. Gresham, Sugai, & Horner (2001) outlined implications for practice in the school setting; they suggested increasing the amount of intervention, providing instruction in the child's natural setting, matching the intervention strategy with the type of skill deficit, and ensuring intervention fidelity to improve the effectiveness of these interventions. Gresham and his colleagues also recommended that social skills interventions be implemented more intensely and frequently than they were delivered to children with social skills deficits at that time. Similarly, Bellini, Peters, Benner, & Hopf (2007) advocated the teaching and reinforcing of social skills as often as possible throughout the school day to increase generalization of acquired skills. Thus, weekly lessons in this curriculum are presented in a varied format to offer many opportunities for generalization.

As the instructor, you hold the key to the success of this program. You are both social interpreter and guide as you model the many specifics and subtleties of social interactions. In these roles, you explain and demonstrate the skills presented in detail and with explanation of complexity. Your lessons are structured to allow for student question and answer exchanges and plenty of chances for modeling and discussion.

As we know, students with ASD often miss key elements in the intent of social interactions, and thus experience difficulties in communicating with others, in processing and integrating information from the environment, in establishing and sustaining social relationships with others, and in participating in new environments (Bellini et al., 2007). Students typically benefit from explicit instruction that is generalized across settings in order to practice social skills that vary according to the situation (Rao, Beidel, & Murray, 2008; Reichow & Volkmar, 2010). For example, when you are teaching students how to make an apology later in this book, in addition to explaining how to do so, you will describe circumstances that warrant an apology and then provide practice utilizing a variety of scenarios.

Unlike many other social skills curricula that call for a lot of supplementation, everything you need for a great, year-long social skills class is right here. All you have to do is facilitate the lessons and make student copies of materials. For the students, this curriculum offers an opportunity to delve into specific social skills topics through scripts and interviews, with plenty of review. As a result, the students learn both about the social skill and about ways to apply it, through generalization, into broader settings through practice skits, interviews at school, and trips into the community. This type of scripted practice helps you prepare students on the spectrum for real-world situations by providing an invaluable way to support their auditory memories through creating visual/action memories in a low-stress environment.

Current research recommends a systematic approach to teaching social skills to promote understanding through repetition (White, Keonig, & Scahill, 2007). Although many students with ASD lack some skills necessary for social cognition, they show a great deal of social interest and benefit from skills taught directly with room for questioning (Myles, Trautman, & Shelvan, 2014).

Recently researchers have reviewed a number of studies of social skills programs and have begun to identify what appears to be effective best practice. Reviewing five studies on social skills groups, for example, researchers at the University of Utah and the University of California, Davis, M.I.N.D. Institute attempted to identify some "essential ingredients" for an effective social skills group (White et al., 2007). These central principles identified are:

- Make abstract concepts concrete
- Provide structure and predictability

- Provide scaffolded language support
- Provide varied and multiple learning opportunities
- Include "other-focused" activities (such that children always work in groups or pairs and such that cooperation and partnership are encouraged)
- Foster self-awareness and self-esteem
- Select relevant goals for most important social skills deficits
- Program in a sequential and progressive manner
- Provide opportunities for programmed generalization and ongoing practice to ensure that the skills are used and useful beyond the group setting

With research and best practice in mind, this curriculum is sure to surpass your expectations. Best of all, students have fun while they learn!

Components of the Book

Each thematic unit includes:

- Social skills warmup activities
- A fun skill explanation that uses three example characters—Jet the Jerk, Timid Timothy, and Mature Matt—to demonstrate the possible approaches to the unit's theme
- An oral true-or-false quiz
- A "thumbs up" and "thumbs down" quiz
- Skits (which can be videotaped for review)
- Guided group discussion questions
- Thematic interviews of people outside the classroom environment
- A cumulative review bingo game

In addition, after every two target units, students will have an opportunity to experience learned skills through field trips or alternative activities at school—such as creating a "classroom restaurant." A review section is provided after every four units in order to reinforce what has been learned.

Unit Structure

Each social skills unit is composed of the following elements.

Daily Check-in and Warm-up Activity

Because individuals with ASD tend to experience high levels of stress (White, Oswald, Ollendick, & Scahill, 2009), each daily lesson begins with a check-in of individual students' mood and affect based on *The Incredible 5-Point Scale* (Buron & Curtis, 2013). According to Attwood (2006), the more a person with ASD understands his or her emotions, the more able that person is to express those emotions appropriately. Thus, the daily check-in system is an essential tool for student self-reflection, with warm-up activities fostering student engagement in a relaxed atmosphere.

Check-in is followed by warm-up topics (see Appendix B for a list) using a talking stick, with students seated on chairs in a circle. This activity is meant to relax the students and to promote communication in a group setting.

Explanation of the Skill

Because social skills must be taught, learned, and performed (Gresham et al., 2001), each social skills unit begins with a skill explanation read by the instructor. This includes explaining why and how the skill is used and provides an opportunity for students to share their personal experiences and background knowledge in the form of a discussion.

Furthermore, because human nature allows us to see others' behaviors clearly—and not necessarily our own until we are ready—this curriculum uses three characters to highlight how a person may display the skill. For example, the character of "Jet the Jerk" is generally uncaring and rude; "Timid Timothy" is a whiner who blames others for negative things that happen to him; and "Mature Matt" demonstrates good decision-making and coping skills in all situations. The goal for students is to become like "Mature Matt." Some students may be at different stages of achieving this, and Jet and Timothy demonstrate skill deficiencies worthy of analysis and discussion.

Group Quizzes: *True or False* and *Thumbs-Up or Thumbs-Down*

The two quizzes allow students to think about a given social skill in a variety of settings and situations. In a sense, they make students think about the skill before being asked to practice it. Students must respond based on whether or not the statement given is socially appropriate. No writing is necessary because students respond with an oral "true" or "false" or a nonverbal "thumbs-up" or "thumbs-down."

Skits

The ability to interpret others' perspectives or beliefs, as well as their thoughts and feelings, across contexts is an essential social skill that is often difficult for people with ASD (Baron-Cohen, 2001; Flavell, 2004). Given the challenges related to this skill, generalization is promoted through role-play techniques that use a variety of scripts and situations. Furthermore, students with ASD often have a strong visual memory but lack the ability to plan for novel events or settings. For these students, role-play techniques help prepare them for social situations (Ramamoorthi & Nelson, 2011). Priming procedures through role-play are used as a way to increase social skills by presenting cognitive or behavioral primes before performance of these skills or behaviors are required in a natural setting (Bellini et al.).

These role-play techniques provide an opportunity for rehearsal of desired behaviors, with checks by the teacher for immediate feedback (Hattie & Timperley, 2007). In short, students practice social situations in a fun environment while given the words to use to express themselves. They demonstrate emotion through acting and, in general, love watching and sharing their videotaped selections.

Generalization

"Teaching generalization is often a problem for children with autism. To teach a child to generalize the principle of not running across the street, it must be taught in many different locations. If he is taught in only one location, the child will think that the rule only applies to one specific place," wrote Temple Grandin (2002). Students learn generalization skills in this curriculum through interviews with school staff as well as through direct practice of skills in the community through periodic field trips.

Review of Information

Review and feedback are essential for retention (Hattie & Timperley). Therefore, students review skills often, through review bingo after every unit, videotaped skits, interview evaluations, and a comprehensive skill review after every four units. Through various activities, students review the same material in a slightly different format, thus keeping the topics interesting and relevant.

How to Use This Book

This book is intended to be used for social skills instruction with students in grades seven through twelve who are either on the autism spectrum or have other related disorders, and who have mid-range skills in social understanding and use of expressive language. I encourage special education teachers, speech-language pathologists, psychologists, and parents to use the book as a tool to guide young people through the intricacies of appropriate social interaction. Through practice of these prescribed skills, students will gain both knowledge and confidence in using the skills across settings with varying groups of people.

Here's What You Do

Daily Check-in and Warm-ups

Arrange chairs so that students are seated in a circle throughout the lesson. Begin by checking in with each student using the five-point scale based on *The Incredible 5-Point Scale* (Buron & Curtis). Say, for example, "Rate how you are feeling today on a scale of one to five" using a chart with the numbers one to five, paired with pictures as a visual. Basically you can use this scale in countless ways, going from a rating of one to five. I often use it just as a way for students to measure their level of calmness daily. I display a big "1–5" chart in my room, including colors and matching facial expressions. One equals very calm, two equals calm, three equals somewhat calm, four equals not very calm, and five equals not calm at all. Encourage the students to tell the group why they may be feeling the way they are feeling and to take care of themselves with support from the group. For example, if a student says, "I am close to a five," the group may ask him or her what might help to calm down, or they could just offer words of support. You may then facilitate helping the student calm down by talking to the student in private or by providing the student with a quiet place to relax before rejoining the group.

Next, complete a "warm-up" activity. You may wish to pass around a talking stick and have each student answer a discussion question found in Appendix B, or do some other activity such as a card game or board game. For the talking stick activity, encourage the students to share just two or three points and then pass the stick along. If a student is unable to monitor the length of his or her conversation, feel free to put a time limit on turns.

Explanation of the Skill

Read the explanation of the day's skill to students with the help of the characters: Jet the Jerk, Timid Timothy, and Mature Matt. Also read the questions highlighted for students in italicized letters to allow for student participation and checks for understanding.

Group Quizzes

Read the true or false and then the thumbs-up or thumbs-down quiz questions to the students, pausing when appropriate for discussion. These quizzes are designed to encourage students to think about the target social skill in a variety of situations. Students listen to each statement and then either call out "true" or "false" or give a clear thumbs-up or thumbs-down. There is no answer key because some of the statements can be either true or false, appropriate or not appropriate, according to the situation. This was done intentionally to illustrate that for many social skills there are no "hard and fast" rules, and your explanation will be invaluable to the students.

Skits

Read the instructions to the students and then ask students to get into pairs to perform the skits. On occasion, skits will involve three student actors, but this is more the exception than the rule. One student in each group should be designated to read the introduction, including plot, setting, and key concepts, before the group begins. At the end of each skit, ask the students to write brief sentences as a form of reflection and accountability. If time allows, have the students practice each skit twice before selecting one skit to be videotaped. Videotape one of each group's selections to be watched sometime that week and/or during the review week. **Copies of the skits are needed for this exercise.**

Group Discussions

Read the instructions to the students. Have students take turns alternating asking the discussion questions while practicing their listening skills. For example, cue students to look at their discussion partner and nod to show interest. Also, as part of this activity, students are to practice and perform a skit for the class. Because this skit is not scripted, they may need support from you if they have questions about content. **Copies of the discussion questions are needed for this exercise.**

Generalization

Read the instructions to the students, practice the questions, and then conduct the interviews—either with guests coming into the room or with students going out to interview staff members. If students are leaving the classroom, be sure to call ahead and ask the staff members when they are available for the interviews. Some staff I have involved over the years include school secretaries, custodians, administration, and related service personnel. They have been wonderful to work with! An added benefit to reaching out to these particular staff members is that students start to form relationships with them and often end up seeking them out at other times of the day. Overall, the purpose of this activity is to generalize social skills to a larger school setting. **Copies of the interviews and rating sheets are needed for this exercise. Make copies of the Interview Review sheets for the students to take to their interviewees and then hand in afterward.**

It is not necessary for students to write down responses from their interviews, but remind them to use appropriate verbal and nonverbal communication skills and to ask their interviewees to complete a rating sheet. Review the evaluations after the interviews, conferencing with each of the students briefly as they submit their completed rating sheets.

Review Bingo

Read the instructions and play bingo. The purpose of the bingo game is to review the skill in a fun way while checking for comprehension through demonstration of skills and verbal input. Decide whether or not to give a small prize to the winners or to play just "for fun." You could also play "blackout" by covering all the spaces or play "five-in-a-row" until either one person or until everyone wins. **Students receive either "Copy A" or "Copy B" of bingo so that everyone does not get the same bingo sheet. Bingo copies for this exercise are found in Appendix A.**

Community Practice

After every two lessons, arrange for students to go out into the community to practice social skills when possible. If this is not possible, alternative activities are included in those sections. Be sure to communicate fully with tour guides, explaining the nature of the group and your objectives. For the students, it may also be helpful to prepare and read a social narrative about expectations before any of these events as well as to watch a Youtube clip of a location similar to the one they will be visiting.

Skills Review

After every four lessons, there is a week-long skill review. Read the instructions each day and monitor students' ability to retain and apply knowledge from past lessons. The purpose of the review is provide variety to the class while reviewing key concepts for retention. Also, at this time students watch videotaped skits of themselves followed by group discussion. Students also may watch video clips of the skills from the Internet. YouTube is often a good resource for these videos. **Bingo copies for this exercise are found in Appendix A.**

Note

Please use discretion in the way you use the scripts. Make sure you sound natural and adjust the wording, as needed, for your particular group of students.

Best wishes to you as you lead your students to mastery of essential social skills! May laughter and emotion fill your classroom as students "get a feel" for how these skills work in a fun, nonthreatening learning environment.

UNIT ONE

SELF-INTRODUCTION

Instructor reads: Today's topic has to do with self-introductions.

Can you think of a time when you made a good self-introduction? (Pause) Would anyone be willing to share what happened? (Students respond; instructors can share as well.)

When introducing yourself, it's good to keep in mind a few characters who can serve as either positive or negative role models.

Character #1 is "Jet the Jerk." Jet never looks interested in meeting anyone. He walks around with a frown on his face and body language that says, "get away from me!" For example, if someone says, "Hi. What's your name?" he usually either doesn't respond or he makes a face at the person and walks away.

What do you think of Jet's behavior? (Students respond.)

Character #2 is "Timid Timothy." Timothy usually looks hunched over and is extremely shy—trying not to be noticed or have anyone interact with him. For example, if someone tries to introduce him- or herself to Timothy, he often looks down at the ground, mumbles something under his breath, and extends a limp hand to shake. He often complains that new people don't want to talk to him, but he makes no effort to talk to others.

What do you think of Timothy's behavior? (Students respond.)

Character #3 is "Mature Matt." Mature Matt is not naturally outgoing, but he does his best to appear friendly and open to meeting new people. For example, if a new person walks into a party, he usually goes up to the person, smiles, and says, "Hi, I'm Matt. What's your name?" Then he asks the person a few questions to try to make him or her feel comfortable.

What do you think of Matt's behavior? (Students respond.)

In this unit we'll be talking a lot about self-introductions. Through practice and self-control, anyone can be like "Mature Matt." The key is to keep working hard on this skill and never give up on yourself. Best wishes to you all!

True or False Quiz

Instructor reads:

1. It is polite to ignore someone when meeting for the first time.
2. People generally form a good impression of someone who smiles and appears interested.
3. You always shake hands when meeting somebody for the first time.
4. People are always interested in what you have to say and will not want to also talk about their interests.
5. When meeting someone for the first time, you should ask the person at least one question.
6. It's OK to be nervous when meeting a new person.
7. In general, it is not OK to point out a person's flaws when meeting them for the first time.
8. It's common to be *overly polite* when meeting somebody for the first time.

Thumbs-Up or Thumbs-Down

Instructor reads:

1. A new kid introduces himself to you and you act *super bored.*
2. An adult comes into the room to meet you for a job interview. You appear *uninterested,* mumble something into your sleeve, and look out the window.
3. Someone you *"like"* walks in. You act very interested and appear overly excited, talking a mile a minute about very personal information.

4. A kid whom you don't know walks in. You introduce yourself and start telling her a lot of very personal information about yourself.
5. When shaking hands with adults, you squeeze their hands so hard that it hurts.
6. An adult whom you don't know walks into your classroom. You politely tell your name and ask for his or hers.
7. A kid walks in carrying a video game that you happen to like. You say "hi" and ask about the game. Shortly thereafter you introduce yourself fully.
8. An adult walks in and you giggle wildly, saying, "It's nice to meet you. It's nice to meet you," in an android voice.

Skits

Instructor reads: Practice the following skits with either one or two classmates. Select one skit to be videotaped by your teacher for the class. Words in **bold** are meant to be read with expression. Brackets are used to give acting directions. One student in each group should read the introduction, including the plot, setting, and key concepts, for each skit before choosing actors to portray each role. Take special note that skits one and three require three characters instead of the usual two, to allow for making an introduction in a small group setting. Have fun!

Skit 1: Meeting Your Dad's Friend, Jack

Students choose one person to read the introduction before choosing characters and practicing the skit.

Introduction

Plot: Dad introduces C.J. to his friend, Jack. The actors are Dad, C.J., and Jack.
Setting: In the kitchen
Key concept: After introducing yourself, ask the other person questions and say, "Oh really?" to keep the conversation going.

Skit

Dad: Hi C.J., I'd like to introduce you to Jack, who's an old friend of mine.

C.J.: Nice to meet you, Jack. [Giving a firm handshake] I'm C.J.
Jack: So, what grade are you in at school, C.J.?
C.J.: I'm in the ninth grade. [Pause] And what do you like to do in your free time?
Jack: Well, I'm a big golfer.
C.J.: Oh, really? [Looking interested]
Jack: **Yeah, it's great!** Perhaps you'll take an interest in it someday. [Smiling] It's fun, and it can be great exercise if you don't spend too much time riding around the course on the golf cart like **your dad here**.
Dad: [Smiling] Now, Jack, I seem to remember **it wasn't me** who crashed that cart last year near par 4.
Jack: **Oh, that?** It was an **accident**! [Laughing] Could have happened to **anyone**.
Dad: Yeah, **right**!
C.J.: Well, I have to get going now, guys. [Getting up to leave.] **It was nice meeting you, Jack.** Have fun with my dad!
Jack: It was nice to meet you, too. [Smiling] You're a **great** kid!
C.J.: Thanks. [Leaving] See ya later!
Jack: Yeah, see you around.
END OF SKIT

Students answer in writing: How does C.J. show politeness in this skit?

Skit 2: Meeting Someone and Making a Poor Impression (What Not to Do)

Students choose one person in each group to read the introduction before choosing characters and practicing the skit.

INTRODUCTION

Plot: C.J. is rude to the substitute teacher, Ms. Allex, and demonstrates what **not** to do when making a first impression. The actors are C.J. and Ms. Allex.
Setting: In the classroom
Key concept: If you ignore someone when meeting them for the first time, that person will most likely view you as someone who is rude.

SKIT

Ms. Allex: [Walking into the classroom.] Oh, hi there. [Looking around] This is a **nice** classroom you have. I'm Ms. Allex, and I'll be the sub today. [Pause] What's your name?

C.J.: [Looking up from the desk and then back down again] **Huh?**
Ms. Allex: Well, I was **asking** your name. [Smiling] I'm Ms. Allex and I'll be working in this classroom for a few days. It's nice to meet you.
C.J.: I don't **like subs**.
Ms. Allex: Well, I didn't care for new staff much either when I was your age, but let's see what we can do to get along, shall we?
C.J.: **Whatever!** [Looking down unhappily]
Ms. Allex: How about if I give you a little time to yourself and then we'll get into the lesson? We'll see you in a bit. [Walking to another part of the classroom]
C.J.: [Staring off in the distance]
END OF SKIT

Students answer in writing: What might Ms. Allex be thinking about C.J. right now and why?

Skit 3: Meeting Someone Who Shares Your Interest in Video Games

Students choose one person in each group to read the introduction before choosing the three characters and practicing the skit.

INTRODUCTION
Plot: Richard introduces A.J. to his friend Patrick. The actors are Richard, A.J., and Patrick.
Setting: In the school cafeteria.
Key concept: Sharing a personal interest sometimes leads to spending more time with the person you have just met.

SKIT
Richard: Hey A.J., How's it going? [Walking over to Patrick with A.J.] A.J., this is Patrick, the guy I was telling you about. [Pause] Patrick is totally into video games like you.
A.J.: Nice to meet you, Patrick. [Smiling] So what kind of games do you like?
Patrick: Oh, the usual. I like *King Kong Wongton* and *Speed Racer Kimono Dragon.*
A.J.: **Really?** I like those, **too**! [Looking excited] My **highest** score was 250,000 for each.
Patrick: You sound pretty good. [Pause] Do you want to come over to my house to play them sometime?

A.J.: [Smiling] Yeah, that sounds great!
Richard: Mind if I join you too?
Patrick: **Yeah, sure.** How about next Friday night at six o'clock?
A.J.: Works for me.
Richard: I don't have anything going on then, so that should be fine.
Patrick: OK. [Getting up to leave] See you then!
A.J.: Bye! [Leaving] See you Friday.
Richard: [Leaving] Yeah, see ya!
END OF SKIT

Students answer in writing: How can you tell that Patrick enjoyed meeting A.J.?

Skit 4: Interviewing for a Job

Students choose one person in each group to read the introduction before choosing characters and practicing the skit.

INTRODUCTION

Plot: A.J. goes to an interview for a summer job at a video store. He meets with the owner of the store, Mr. Jorgenson. The actors are A.J. and Mr. Jorgenson.
Setting: In Mr. Jorgenson's office
Key concept: When at a job interview, try to convince the person who is interviewing you that you would be a good person for the job.

SKIT

Mr. Jorgenson: Hi! [Extending a hand to shake] I'm Rick Jorgenson, the owner of Video 4U.
A.J.: [Shaking hands.] Oh, hi. I'm A.J. [Smiling] It's very nice to meet you.
Mr. Jorgenson: It's nice to meet you, too. [Pause and lean back] So A.J., tell me why you would like to work here.
A.J.: [Smiling] Well, I really enjoy playing video games. I know a lot about them, and I also have some experience in sales. Last year I sold magazines for a school fundraiser, and I got the top prize for selling the most subscriptions. You could say I'm a real "people person."
Mr. Jorgenson: Well, it sounds like you're **just the kind of person this company needs!** You can start on Monday. [Standing up] Just fill out the paperwork with my secretary on your way out.

A.J.: **Thank you, Mr. Jorgenson!** [Standing up, shaking hands with Mr. Jorgenson.] You **won't** be disappointed with this decision!
Mr. Jorgenson: Now, if you'll excuse me, I have a lunch date with my daughter, so I must be going. It was nice meeting you. [Leaving] I think this will work out just great.
A.J.: It was nice meeting you, too. [Leaving] And **thanks again**, sir.
Mr. Jorgenson: Yeah, see you soon! Goodbye!
END OF SKIT

Students answer in writing: Why do you think A.J. got the job?

Group Discussion

Instructor reads: Answer the following questions orally with a partner, then read the steps and design a skit to present to the class.

- When might you introduce yourself to others? Think of at least three situations.
- What is a good way to introduce yourself? What should you do?
- What *shouldn't* you do or say when introducing yourself for the first time?
- Why are first impressions important?
- What *can* you do to make a good first impression?
- Demonstrate a good handshake.
- Demonstrate your own self-introduction as if you didn't know your partner.

ORIGINAL SKIT
Step 1: Choose a scene in which you introduce yourself politely. Think about different possibilities, including meeting a prospective boss, an adult in the building, or a potential friend.
Step 2: Create the skit.
Step 3: Practice the skit.
Step 4: Tell the audience who the actors are, where the scene takes place, and what the skit is about. Perform the skit for the class.

Generalization

Instructor reads: It's time for interviews! First pick a partner and practice your interview script one time. I will then inform you who you will be interviewing—options include school personnel, teachers, and other students. Either I will have set up an appointment to interview someone in the building, or someone will join us today to be interviewed in the room. Next, complete the interview and ask the person you talked with to rate your interviewing skills on your rating sheets. Last, hand in your rating sheets to me, and we will have a quick conference about how things went.

The Interview

Student: [Walking up to the person] Excuse me. Do you have a few minutes to help me with a social skills assignment on **making a good self-introduction?**
Student: [If the person says **"no"**] Thank you anyway.
Student: [If the person says **"yes"**] It won't take long, and at the end I will ask you to rate me on a scale of one to five according to how well I do. Now, please pretend that I am a new student at this school who is meeting you for the first time. I will take part "A," so please take part "B." **Let's begin.**

A: Hi! My name is ______________________________ and I'll be a new student at this school starting next week. [Shake hands.]
B: Hi! It's nice to meet you.
A: It's nice to meet you, too.
B: Where are you from?
A: I'm from ______________________. Where are you from originally?
B: I'm from ______________________.
A: That's nice.
B: Well, it was nice meeting you. I hope you'll enjoy being a student here. We have a great school!
A: Thanks. It was nice to meet you, too! [Leaving.] See you around.
Student: **Thank you.** Now please write your name on the line and rate me on a scale of one to five (one equals poor and five equals excellent), adding comments if you'd like.

Interview Rating

Student's Name ______________________________

Person's Name: ______________________________

Date: ____________________

1. Was I polite when I approached you? _______ (1–5)
2. Did I show that I was listening with my body (using eye contact and standing up straight?) ______ (1–5)
3. Did I use a nice speaking voice? ______ (1–5)
4. Did I make a favorable impression in general? ______ (1–5)

Total score is ______ out of a possible 20.

COMMENTS: ______________________________

Bingo

Instructor reads: It's time for bingo. First I will read off a number and then call on one of you to give an answer, make a comment, or demonstrate a skill. Everyone can cross off the numbers on the bingo sheets as they are called. You win by getting five in a row. Good luck to you all!

1. Demonstrate a good handshake.
2. Demonstrate a poor handshake (what not to do).
3. Demonstrate looking bored when meeting someone—what not to do!
4. What words can you use when introducing yourself?
5. What is an example of something you shouldn't say to a person you've just met?
6. Give two examples of who you might introduce yourself to.
7. Give two examples of where you might meet someone new.
8. What questions could you ask another student when meeting them for the first time?
9. What can you say to a person you've just met when that person starts to leave?
10. What question could you ask an adult you've just met?
11. What three things make for a good first impression?
12. What can you say if a person you've just met asks you what your interests are?
13. How can you limit yourself from only talking about your interests when meeting someone for the first time?
14. Demonstrate how you would introduce yourself to a new teacher.
15. Demonstrate how you would introduce yourself to a new student.
16. What words can you use to ask a person what his or her interests are?
17. Demonstrate good body language when making a self-introduction. What would your body communicate to people in this case?
18. What was your favorite skit in this unit and why?

19. Tell about two common mistakes some people make during a self-introduction.
20. What are three things you could say about yourself when meeting a new teacher?
21. What two things wouldn't you share when meeting someone for the first time?
22. What kind of person would you like to be friends with, who you haven't met yet?
23. Time for a skit! Pick a partner and perform a short skit. Plot: Someone about your age moves into your neighborhood. You bring a plate of cookies over and introduce yourself at the door. The actors are you and a new neighbor.
24. Problem solving: Eric has a problem. Whenever he meets a new person he shows little interest in what the person has to say and dominates the conversation by going on and on about his latest video game. List three ways Eric can solve his problem, including one negative and two positive solutions.

UNIT TWO

CONVERSATION SKILLS

Instructor reads: Today's topic has to do with having a conversation.

Can you think of a time when you had a good conversation with someone? (Pause) Would anyone be willing to share what happened? (Students respond; instructors can share as well.)

When having a conversation, it's good to keep in mind a few characters who can serve as either positive or negative role models.

Character #1 is "Jet the Jerk." Jet never asks questions when he's having a conversation, but simply talks on and on about whatever he's interested in. He loves to talk about how good he is at playing video games, and that's all he really ever wants to discuss. For example, if someone tries to talk about his or her interests, he usually either tries to bring the conversation back to video games or just completely ignores the person.

What do you think of Jet's behavior? (Students respond.)

Character #2 is "Timid Timothy." Timothy usually looks like he doesn't want to talk to anyone, and if someone comes up to talk to him, he freezes and acts like he doesn't have a thing to say. For example, if someone starts a conversation with Timothy, he looks away and half-heartedly answers questions but never asks any questions himself. He later complains, "No one ever wants to talk to me. They're all so mean!"

What do you think of Timothy's behavior? (Students respond.)

Character #3 is "Mature Matt." Mature Matt doesn't mind talking to anyone who wants to have a conversation. He's really good at both listening and at asking questions, and other people like to talk to him. For example, if someone starts talking to Matt, he smiles, nods occasionally, and asks a question or two before moving on to something he likes to talk about.

What do you think of Matt's behavior? (Students respond.)

In this unit, we'll be talking a lot about having good conversations. Through practice and self-control, anyone can be like "Mature Matt." The key is to keep working hard on this skill and to never give up on yourself. Best wishes to you all!

True or False Quiz

Instructor reads:

1. Being a good listener is important when having a conversation.
2. A person generally likes it when you ask questions in a conversation.
3. It's important to look interested in the person who is speaking in a conversation.
4. People usually get bored quickly if the person they are talking to either does not let them talk or does not show any interest in what they are saying.
5. If someone asks, "How was your weekend?" the person generally does not want to hear every single detail of it.
6. Often when an acquaintance asks, "How are you today?" the person is just being polite and expects a short answer like, "Fine, and you?"
7. You can tell that a person is not interested in a conversation if he or she looks bored, yawns, or starts looking around the room.
8. Only really outgoing people are capable of having great conversations with others.

Thumbs-Up or Thumbs-Down

Instructor reads:

1. A friend of yours wants to talk about camping. Even though you are not interested in camping, you ask some questions about it because it's your friend's interest.
2. Someone comes up to you at a party and talks about his or her interests only, without asking you any questions.

3. Someone you just met gives you some information about herself or himself and then asks questions about you.
4. You ask an acquaintance about what his hobbies are, and the person talks and on and on about the topic until you want to scream.
5. You show by the look on your face that you are interested in the conversation you are having with a teacher.
6. You know your friend's mom really likes to bake. When you see her, you often ask her what she's been baking lately.
7. In the middle of a conversation with someone, you suddenly start to stare at either your watch or the clock on the wall.
8. You never look at anyone who is talking to you.

Skits

Instructor reads: Practice the following skits with a classmate. Select one skit to be videotaped by your teacher for the class. Words in **bold** are meant to be read with expression. Brackets are used to give acting directions. One student in each group should read the introduction, including the plot, setting, and key concepts, for each skit before choosing actors to portray each role. Good luck!

Skit 1: Talking to a Friend about Bowling

Students choose one person to read the introduction before choosing characters and practicing the skit.

INTRODUCTION

Plot: A.J. is very excited to talk about bowling. J.J. listens attentively. The actors are A.J. and J.J.

Setting: In the classroom

Key concept: In a conversation, ask the other person questions and say, "Oh really?" to keep the conversation going.

SKIT

A.J.: Hi J.J. [Pause] Did you hear that I went **bowling** last weekend?

J.J.: [Looking interested] **Oh really?** Where did you go?
A.J: Down to the High Way Lanes. [With enthusiasm] I went there on Saturday night and bowled a 250, my **best game ever**.
J.J.: **Wow! That's great!** [Pause] Have you been bowling for a long time?
A.J.: Ever since I was about four years old. I love it! [Pause] By the way, what did you do last weekend?
J.J.: Not much. [Pause] I just hung out and played video games. It was pretty cool though.
A.J.: Yeah, that sounds fun too! [Class is beginning, so the conversation ends.]
END OF SKIT

Students answer in writing: How did J.J. keep this conversation going?

Skit 2: Having a Casual Conversation at a Restaurant

Students choose one person in each group to read the introduction before choosing characters and practicing the skit.

INTRODUCTION

Plot: J.J. is out of town and is getting something to eat at a restaurant before attending a baseball game. He notices Jenna from school, so he walks over to say "hi." The actors are J.J. and Jenna.
Setting: In a restaurant
Key concept: When having a casual conversation, keep it friendly and brief.

SKIT

J.J.: [Walking over to Jenna] Hi, Jenna. How's it going?
Jenna: [Smiling] Good. **And you?**
J.J.: Not too bad. I'm just here with my family getting something to eat before we go to the Twins' game.
Jenna: Oh, really? We're going there, too. We have **great seats**. [Pause] I'm so excited to see the game.
J.J.: Yeah. It's always a good time. Well, I'd better get back to my table, but I just wanted to stop by to say "hi." **Enjoy the game.** [Leaving to return to his table]
Jenna: Yeah. You, too! See you back at school.
J.J.: Yeah. See ya! [Walking away]
END OF SKIT

Students answer in writing: How does J.J. show that he is a polite person?

Skit 3: Talking to a Friend about a New Video Game

Students choose one person in each group to read the introduction before choosing characters and practicing the skit.

INTRODUCTION

Plot: A.J. is very excited to talk about a new video game. C.J. is **not** so interested in the topic, however, and soon gets bored with the conversation. The actors are C.J. and A.J. This general plot will be used in the next skit also, but with a different outcome.
Setting: In the classroom
Key concept: If one person dominates a conversation and won't let the other person talk, the conversation usually ends with one person getting frustrated.

SKIT

A.J.: [Sitting by C.J.] Hey C.J., I'm **totally excited** because I get to play my new video game this weekend.
C.J.: That sounds fun. [Pause] I'm not really planning to do too much this weekend. Maybe I'll just hang around the house ... I don't know.
A.J.: And I can probably stay up most of the night. [Talking quickly] I just got a new game last night. It's called *The Dream Weavers' Web of Destruction* and it's **so cool**!
C.J.: Wow. [Looking a little bored] I haven't even heard of that one, but if you like it, that's great.
A.J.: Oh, it's totally great! [Talking even more excitedly] My last score was 280,000, and I'm going for my all-time high record of 300,000. **I think I can do it.**
C.J.: Well, [staring off] I'll just be hanging around home and maybe watching a video. [Pause] Do you have one I can borrow, by the way?
A.J.: No, not really. [Pause] I think I can make the 300,000 points at about midnight if I really work on it.
C.J.: Well, good luck with that. [Starting to leave] See ya around.
A.J.: See ya. And by the way, I can start playing at about four o'clock—right when I get home.
C.J.: [Getting angry] All right already! Go play your game! I get it!
END OF SKIT

Students answer in writing: What should A.J. have done to make this conversation more interesting to C.J.?

Skit 4: Talking Too Much and Then Changing the Topic

Students choose one person in each group to read the introduction before choosing characters and practicing the skit.

INTRODUCTION

Plot: Once again A.J. is very excited to talk about a new video game. C.J. is not so interested in the topic, however, and soon gets bored. This time A.J. realizes this and changes the subject. The actors are C.J. and A.J.
Setting: In the classroom
Key concept: A person who is dominating the conversation can change the situation by asking questions about the other person's interests.

SKIT

A.J.: [Sitting by C.J.] Hey. I'm **totally excited** because I get to play my new game this weekend called *The Dream Weaver's Web of Destruction.*
C.J.: That sounds fun. I'm not really too into games, but if you like it, that's cool.
A.J.: Well, I'll probably be up most of the night playing—it's going to be awesome.
C.J.: [Looking slightly bored] Hmm. Interesting.
A.J.: [Looking at C.J.] So anyway. [Pause] Enough about me, what have you been up to lately?
C.J.: Well, actually I just got a new science kit in the mail that I'm super excited to try. It's going to be so **awesome** ... if I could just figure out how to set it up.
A.J.: Hey, I'm pretty good at that kind of stuff. Would you like some help?
C.J.: Sure, that would be **great**. Can you stop over about six tonight? [Pause] Then you can tell me more about your game, too.
A.J.: [Smiling] That sounds good. See you at six!
C.J.: [Starts to walk away] See ya then!
END OF SKIT

Students answer in writing: What did A.J. do to include C.J. in on the conversation?

Group Discussion

Instructor reads: Answer the following questions orally with a partner, then read the steps and design a skit to present to the class.

- When is it easy to have a conversation with someone?
- When is it difficult to have a conversation with someone?
- What can you politely say or do when you are *not* interested in what someone is talking about?
- What can you talk about, in general, with someone in a social situation—like when you're at a party?
- How can you tell that someone isn't interested in the topic you are talking about?
- What are some topics your friends like to talk about?
- Demonstrate how you start a conversation with a friend.
- Demonstrate how you start a conversation with a teacher at school.

<u>Original Skit</u>

Step 1: Choose a scene in which you have a conversation with someone. Think about different possibilities, including meeting someone new, talking with someone you're friends with, or talking with an adult.
Step 2: Create the skit.
Step 3: Practice the skit.
Step 4: Tell the audience who the actors are, where the scene takes place, and what the skit is about. Perform the skit for the class.

Generalization

Instructor reads: It's time for interviews! First pick a partner and practice your interview script one time. I will then inform you who you will be interviewing—options include school personnel, teachers, and other students. Either I will have set up an appointment to interview someone in the building or someone will join us today to be interviewed in the room. Next, complete the interview and ask the person you talked with to rate your interviewing skills on your rating sheets. Last, hand in your rating sheets to me, and we will have a quick conference about how things went.

The Interview

Student: [Walking up to the person] Excuse me. Do you have a few minutes to help me with a social skills assignment on **conversation skills**?
Student: [If the person says **"no"**] Thank you anyway.
Student: [If the person says **"yes"**] It won't take long, and at the end I will ask you to rate me on a scale of one to five according to how well I do. I won't write anything down, by the way, so I can concentrate on what you are saying. **Let's begin.**
Student: How can you tell when someone is truly **listening** to you in a conversation?
Student: Could you tell me a little about the **opposite** of having a good conversation? What usually happens?
Student: Why is it important to ask questions when having a conversation?
Student: **Thank you.** Now please write your name on the line and rate me on a scale of one to five (one equals poor and five equals excellent).

Interview Rating

Student's Name ____

Person's Name: ____

Date: ____________________

1. Was I polite when I approached you? ______ (1–5)
2. Did I show that I was listening with my body (using eye contact and standing up straight?) _____ (1–5)
3. Did I use a nice speaking voice? _____ (1–5)
4. Did I make a favorable impression in general? _____ (1–5)

Total score is _____ out of a possible 20.

COMMENTS: ____

Bingo

Instructor reads: It's time for bingo. First I will read off a number and then call on one of you to give an answer, make a comment, or demonstrate a skill. Everyone can cross off the numbers on the bingo sheets as they are called. You win by getting five in a row. Good luck to you all!

1. *Why* is it important to be a good listener when having a conversation?
2. Tell two things to keep in mind when having a good conversation.
3. Name one topic you could talk about with someone your own age.
4. Name one topic you could talk about with an adult you know.
5. What are the reasons for having good conversations?
6. *When* could you have a conversation with someone?
7. *Where* you could you have a conversation with someone?
8. What words could you politely use to ask about someone's interests?
9. What words could you politely say to *excuse yourself* from a conversation that doesn't interest you?
10. What are some topics that your teachers like to talk about?
11. What could you do if the person you are talking to is going on and on about a topic that doesn't interest you?
12. What questions would you ask a classmate to find out about his or her interests?
13. What was your favorite skit in this unit and why?
14. What is one thing you could talk a lot about?
15. What is one topic to *avoid,* in general, when having a conversation?
16. Give an example of what two people might talk about at school.
17. Give an example of what two people might talk about at home.
18. Give an example of what two people might talk about in the community.
19. Do you know anyone who is a good at having conversations? If so, how does that person act?
20. Why is it important to look *interested* when having a conversation?

21. *Problem solving:* Chuck has a problem. He keeps trying to have a conversation with his friends about his new video game, but they don't appear to be listening. List three ways Chuck can solve his problem, including one negative and two positive solutions.
22. *Time for a skit!* Pick a partner and perform a short skit. **Plot:** You are at a party and you meet someone you'd like to talk to. You introduce yourself and ask the person some get-to-know-you questions. The actors are you and the person you want to talk to.
23. *Time for a skit!* Pick a partner and perform a short skit. **Plot:** You are at school and a new student comes into class carrying a game that you really like. You walk over and talk to the student politely. The actors are you and the new kid.
24. *Problem solving:* Mari has a problem. Whenever she tries to have a conversation, she bores the other person by talking about only what **she** wants to talk about. List three ways Mari can solve her problem, including one negative and two positive solutions.

COMMUNITY PRACTICE

Instructor Preparation for the Tour

1. Choose a place to visit in the community and arrange for a tour. Explain who your group is, what they will do there, and what they hope to learn. Options include a store, a bank, a hotel, a police station, a hospital, or a local newspaper.
2. Discuss with the class what to expect to see on the tour and review behavioral expectations.
3. If possible, watch a short video to preview a place similar to the one you will be visiting. (YouTube is a good resource for short videos.)
4. Instruct the students to practice self-introductions.
5. Instruct the students to think of and practice two questions they might ask of the guide while on the tour.
6. Designate a student leader to give the initial greetings and the closing remarks while on the tour.

Student Expectations During the Tour

1. When arriving, the student leader says to the guide, "Hi! We're here for the tour."
2. All students then make an introduction, starting with the student leader.

3. All students ask two questions of the guide, one at the beginning and the other at some point throughout the tour.
4. At the end, the student leader says, "Thank you for the tour."
5. All students write thank you notes and send them to the guide.

Option for Self-Introduction Practice Without Taking a Tour

Invite school staff members whom students either don't know, or don't know well, to come to your room for one class. Examples of people to invite include teachers, paraprofessionals, administrators, custodians, cooks, and coaches. Explain to the guests how the class will be structured. Students should be seated around the room next to an empty chair. Guests will be welcomed in and will be asked to sit next to a student. Set a timer for two minutes, allowing for both the student and the guest to give an introduction and share a bit about themselves. Students should be cued to ask two questions of the guest, such as "Where are you from originally?" and "What do you like to do in your free time?" When the timer goes off, guests will be asked to move clockwise around the room. When the students have met all the guests, the students will thank the guests for coming and sit back down in their chairs. This will be a good time to review how the introductions went and what students learned about the guests. Students could then also write follow-up cards thanking the guests for coming.

UNIT THREE

APOLOGY "DOS" AND "DON'TS"

Instructor reads: Today's topic has to do with making an apology.

Can you think of a time when you made a good apology? (Pause) Would anyone be willing to share what happened? (Students respond; instructors can share as well.)

When making an apology, it's good to keep in mind a few characters who can serve as either positive or negative role models.

Character #1 is "Jet the Jerk." Jet never apologizes about anything. He thinks nothing is ever his fault, and he blames everyone else for his mistakes. For example, say Jet hurt someone's feelings or broke something that didn't belong to him. Most likely he wouldn't care that he did it and may even say something rude, like "Who cares? It's not my problem."

What do you think of Jet's behavior? (Students respond.)

Character #2 is "Timid Timothy." Timothy is a really good person, but he lets people walk all over him. If he does even the slightest thing wrong, he over-apologizes, takes the blame for everything, and lets everyone know his drama. For example, if someone bumped into him in the lunch room he would apologize loudly over and over—even though it wasn't his fault—and announce that he was "stupid."

What do you think of Timothy's behavior? (Students respond.)

Character #3 is "Mature Matt." Mature Matt is a pretty calm and thoughtful guy. If he does something wrong, he accepts responsibility and makes a good apology. For example, if Matt breaks a friend's phone on accident, he says he's sorry and makes sure he pays for it. If he makes a mistake, he apologizes right away.

What do you think of Matt's behavior? (Students respond.)

In this unit we'll be talking a lot about apologies. Through practice and self-control, the goal is to become like "Mature Matt." The key is to keep working hard on the skill and never give up on yourself. Best wishes to you all!

True or False Quiz

Instructor reads:

1. It is always important to apologize for *everything* that goes wrong.
2. When making a sincere apology, it is best to wait until you are *calm*.
3. It feels *good* when someone apologizes sincerely to you after making a mistake.
4. During a sincere apology, the person apologizing usually rolls his or her eyes as if to say, "This is *stupid*."
5. If the tone of voice used in an apology is *sincere*, the apology is usually sincere.
6. It is *common* for people to apologize after a minor accident or mistake.
7. People who grow up in families that don't apologize can *never* learn to apologize.
8. People sometimes say "I'm sorry" even when they don't really mean it, just to be *polite*.

Thumbs-Up or Thumbs-Down

Instructor reads:

1. You forget your friend's birthday. When you see him or her later in the day, you apologize by saying, "I'm *really sorry* I forgot about your birthday. I'll make it up to you!"
2. You are one hour late to work. You see your boss near the office and say, "Sorry I couldn't make it in earlier; *it happens*," with a rude tone of voice with no further explanation.

3. A friend is saddened by your hurtful comments. Instead of sincerely apologizing, you shrug your shoulders and say in a rude tone of voice, "Sorry. *Now get over it.*"
4. Someone makes you really mad. You blow up, yell at the person, and say insulting things. When you are asked to apologize you say, "I'm sorry that *you're such an idiot.*"
5. You're at the grocery store, and your shopping cart lightly strikes someone else's cart. You tearfully shout, "Wow! I am so sorry. *How could I be so stupid?* Please forgive me. It will *never* happen again!"
6. You apologize politely to your math teacher for forgetting to do an assignment.
7. Your boss, Judy, makes a mistake and then *yells* at you in front of your coworkers. When she realizes her error, she apologizes to you in private and then tells the others it was really her mistake.
8. A neighbor's dad recently died. When you see your neighbor going out to get the mail, you walk up to him and say, *"I'm sorry to hear of your loss."*

Skits

Instructor reads: Practice the following skits with a classmate. Select one skit to be videotaped by your teacher for the class. Words in **bold** are meant to be read with expression. Brackets are used to give acting directions. One student in each group should read the introduction, including the plot, setting, and key concepts, for each skit before choosing actors to portray each role. Good luck!

Skit 1: Forgetting an Appointment with a Friend

Students choose one person to read the introduction before choosing characters and practicing the skit.

INTRODUCTION

Plot: C.J. is supposed to meet A.J. in a restaurant at noon but arrives an hour late. The actors are C.J. and A.J.

Setting: At the restaurant

Key concept: When making a mistake, give a sincere apology and try to make up for the error.

SKIT

C.J.: [Rushing up to A.J. at the table] **Oh my gosh! A.J.** I am **so sorry** that I am showing up this **late**! I should have been here an hour ago, but I totally forgot about it until just now. **I'm really, really sorry!**

A.J.: [Looking angry] Well, I've been **sitting here waiting** and **wondering**. I started thinking that you either forgot about me altogether or that you had gotten into an accident or something.

C.J.: [Looking very sorry] Oh, that's **terrible**. [Pause] I feel **so badly** about this. It's totally my fault. I just can't seem to keep things straight these days. How about if I make it up to you by buying your lunch?

A.J.: [Looking surprised] **Really?** [Pause] You know you don't have to do that.

C.J.: But I **want** to. [Pause] It's the **least** I can do. What do you say?

A.J.: [Smiling] Well, all right then. If you insist.

C.J.: [Smiling] I insist, and next time, I'll meet you **right** on time.

A.J.: Sounds good to me.

C.J.: You're not mad at me then?

A.J.: No, I'm not mad. [Pause] Now let's get something to eat. I'm **starving**.

C.J.: Me too!

END OF SKIT

Students answer in writing: How does C.J. make A.J. feel better?

Skit 2: Accidently Bumping into a Jerk

Students choose one person to read the introduction before choosing characters and practicing the skit.

INTRODUCTION

Plot: C.J. accidentally bumps into a stranger while standing in line at the movie theater. The stranger reacts poorly. The actors are C.J. and the stranger.

Setting: In line at the movie theater

Key concept: Not everyone you are polite to is polite to you in return. What *is* important is that you stay calm and do the right thing.

SKIT

C.J.: [Bumping into a stranger in line] Oh gee! **Sorry,** I didn't mean to bump you.

Stranger: [Acting angry and very upset] Why don't you look where you're going, jerk?

C.J.: [Using a nice tone of voice] I'm sorry. [Pause] It was an accident. Please excuse me.

Stranger: [Using a rude tone of voice] You should be more **careful** next time.

C.J.: [Shrugging and getting back in line] Well, everyone makes mistakes.

END OF SKIT

Students answer in writing: How did C.J. show self-control even when the stranger was being rude?

Skit 3: When Someone's Not Quite Ready to Fully Accept an Apology

Students choose one person to read the introduction before choosing characters and practicing the skit.

INTRODUCTION

Plot: J.J. has done something to hurt A.J.'s feelings. They meet the next day, but A.J. is not yet willing to forgive J.J. The actors are A.J. and J.J.

Setting: In the hallway at school

Key concept: When making an apology, timing is important. Sometimes you have to wait until the other person is ready to hear what you have to say.

SKIT

J.J.: [Walking up to A.J.] Hi there, A.J. How's it going?

A.J.: [Angry] Oh, like you care.

J.J.: Look, I acted like a real jerk yesterday, and I'm sorry. I said some things out of anger that I really didn't mean, and I'm truly sorry about that. [Pause] I was wrong, and I wish I could take it all back.

A.J.: [Somewhat calmer, but still a bit angry] Yeah, you **sure** weren't very nice. And I didn't even do anything to start it.

J.J.: **You're right.** I was upset with my mom for grounding me, and I took it out on you. **I'm really sorry.** [Pause] I shouldn't have done that.

A.J.: [Pause] Well, I'm going to need some time to get over this. Thanks for apologizing though.
J.J.: OK, I understand. Sorry again.
A.J.: That's OK. [Pause] See you around.
J.J.: Yeah. See ya. [Turns and walks down the hall]
END OF SKIT

Students answer in writing: Why might A.J. need some time to forgive J.J.?

Skit 4: Saying "Sorry" to the Teacher

Students choose one person to read the introduction before choosing characters and practicing the skit.

INTRODUCTION
Plot: C.J. has forgotten to hand in an assignment to his math teacher, Ms. Bentson. The actors are C.J. and Ms. Bentson (although you can substitute one of your actual teachers' names if you'd like).
Setting: In the classroom at school
Key concept: When making an apology for something you neglected to do, stick to the point and don't make excuses.

SKIT
C.J.: [Entering the classroom] Ms. Bentson, do you have a minute to talk?
Ms. Bentson: Sure, C.J. [Smiling] What's up?
C.J.: I am **so sorry**, but I **just realized** I forgot to hand in my assignment yesterday. I had it done, but I forgot to get it out of my bookbag and put it in the box.
Ms. Bentson: Oh, really?
C.J.: Yeah. I'm wondering if I can **still** hand it in. [Handing her a piece of paper] I mean, I understand if points are taken off for late work, but would you still accept it anyway?
Ms. Bentson: Well, C.J., today is your **lucky** day. I wasn't even going to count the assignment toward anyone's grade. I just wanted to make sure you understood the material. [Looking at the paper] From what I can see of your work, you understood it very well. **Good job!**
C.J.: [Smiling] Well, thanks. What a relief. I was **so worried**!

Ms. Bentson: [Smiling] No problem. Just remember to hand in your work at the end of each class period so this doesn't happen again. Have a good day.
C.J.: [Leaving the room] Yeah thanks, you, too!
END OF SKIT

Students answer in writing: How did C.J. make the apology without making excuses?

Group Discussion

Instructor reads: Answer the following questions orally with a partner, then read the steps and design a skit to present to the class.

- When is it difficult to apologize? Give two examples.
- What is a good way to apologize? What should you do?
- What shouldn't you do when making an apology?
- Why might people say "sorry" when they make small mistakes such as bumping into someone in line?
- Do you think you apologize too much, too little, or just right? Explain.
- How does it feel when someone makes a sincere apology to you? Give one example.
- Tell of a time when you apologized to someone.

ORIGINAL SKIT

Step 1: Choose a scene in which you make a good apology. Think about different possibilities, including apologizing to a parent, a friend, a teacher, or a boss.
Step 2: Create the skit.
Step 3: Practice the skit.
Step 4: Tell the audience who the actors are, where the scene takes place, and what the skit is about. Perform the skit for the class.

Generalization

Instructor reads: It's time for interviews! First pick a partner and practice your interview script one time. I will then inform you who you will be interviewing—options include school personnel, teachers, and other students. Either I will have set up an appointment to interview someone in the building or someone will join us today to be interviewed in the room. Next, complete the interview and ask the person you talked with to rate your interviewing skills on your rating sheets. Last, hand in your rating sheets to me, and we will have a quick conference about how things went.

The Interview

Student: [Walking up to the person] Excuse me. Do you have a few minutes to help me with a social skills assignment on **making an apology**?
Student: [If the person says **"no"**] Thank you anyway.
Student: [If the person says **"yes"**] It won't take long, and at the end I will ask you to rate me on a scale of one to five according to how well I do. I won't write anything down, by the way, so I can concentrate on what you are saying. **Let's begin.**
Student: **When** do you apologize to others? Can you give me some examples?
Student: **Why** do you apologize to others?
Student: How does it feel when someone sincerely apologizes to you for a mistake?
Student: **Thank you.** Now please write your name on the line and rate me on a scale of one to five (one equals poor and five equals excellent), adding comments if you'd like to.

Interview Rating

Student's Name ______________________________

Person's Name: ______________________________

Date: ____________________

1. Was I polite when I approached you? _______ (1–5)
2. Did I show that I was listening with my body (using eye contact and standing up straight?) ______ (1–5)
3. Did I use a nice speaking voice? ______ (1–5)
4. Did I make a favorable impression in general? ______ (1–5)

Total score is ______ out of a possible 20.

COMMENTS: ______________________________

Bingo

Instructor reads: It's time for bingo. First I will read off a number and then call on one of you to give an answer, make a comment, or demonstrate a skill. Everyone can cross off the numbers on the bingo sheets as they are called. You win by getting five in a row. Good luck to you all!

1. Demonstrate in words a *poor* way to apologize (what *not* to do).
2. Tell two things that make for a good apology.
3. Demonstrate polite body language and tone of voice as you say, "I'm sorry."
4. Demonstrate polite body language and tone of voice as you say, "Excuse me."
5. What words should you use when making an apology?
6. What shouldn't you say when making an apology?
7. Give two examples of circumstances in which you might make an apology.
8. Give an example of what words to use when *over-apologizing* for a simple mistake (what *not* to do).
9. How can you tell that your apology has been accepted?
10. What was your favorite skit in this unit and why?
11. Why shouldn't you try to apologize when you're angry?
12. What words do young children use to apologize?
13. What words would you use to apologize to your new boss after you show up late for work twice in a row?
14. Tell us about someone who gives sincere apologies. How does that person act?
15. Should you apologize at a time when someone is very angry with you? Explain.
16. How can you make it up to someone if you broke something?
17. In general, *when* is it a good time to apologize?
18. In general, *why* do we apologize?
19. Why do you think people say "I'm sorry for your loss" at a funeral?

20. What makes for an *insincere* apology?
21. Is it OK to write a note of apology instead of telling someone you're sorry?
22. *Time for a skit!* Pick a partner and perform a short skit. **Plot:** Apologize to a teacher for handing in your work late. Also ask if you can still hand it in. The actors are you and the teacher.
23. *Time for a skit!* Pick a partner and perform a short skit. **Plot:** Pretend you are driving a car and accidentally run into another car. Get out of the car and apologize to the other driver. The actors are you and the other driver.
24. *Problem solving:* Manuel has a problem. Whenever he apologizes, he looks angry and uses a rude tone of voice. List three ways Manuel can solve his problem, including one negative and two positive solutions.

UNIT FOUR

SELF-ADVOCACY

Instructor reads: Today's topic has to do with self-advocacy.

Self-advocacy *means telling others about a need while using a polite tone of voice. Can you think of a time when you were a good self-advocate? (Pause) Would anyone be willing to share what happened? (Students respond; instructors can share as well.)*

When thinking about self-advocacy, it's good to keep in mind a few characters who can serve as either positive or negative role models.

Character #1 is "Jet the Jerk." Jet *never* asks for what he needs politely. Rather, he often yells, makes demands, and gets angry in an effort to get his way. This works some of the time, but a lot of the time he doesn't get what he needs because of his approach. For example, say Jet can't hear what the teacher is saying in class because his classmates are talking too loudly. In this case he would most likely stand up and yell something like, "Why don't you all just *shut up*!" This might make his classmates laugh and get *him* in trouble for disrupting class.

What do you think of Jet's behavior? (Students respond.)

Character #2 is "Timid Timothy." When Timothy has a need, he usually doesn't just say what he needs, but rather, he whines and complains and hints around about it. For example, if he would like something to eat while visiting relatives, he doesn't ask for food but says things like, "I'm so hungry, I wish I had something to eat!" or he simply complains that his stomach is growling, hoping they will figure out what he needs.

What do you think of Timothy's behavior? (Students respond.)

Character #3 is "Mature Matt." Mature Matt most often keeps his cool and calmly asks for the things he needs. He knows the difference between something he can wait for and something he can't. When he has a true need, he thinks about what he can do about it and figures out a plan. For example, if Matt gets overwhelmed and needs a break from class at school, he quietly explains to the teacher that he needs to step out of the room and get a drink to clear his head.

What do you think of Matt's behavior? (Students respond.)

In this unit we'll be talking a lot about self-advocacy. Through practice and self-control, anyone can be like "Mature Matt." The key is to keep working hard on the skill and never give up on yourself. Best wishes to you all!

True or False Quiz

Instructor reads:

1. Only chronic *complainers* ask for what they need from others.
2. Self-advocacy means asking for *too many* favors.
3. An example of self-advocacy is when someone tells a mean kid to *leave him alone.*
4. Being a good self-advocate means you *always* get what you want.
5. An example of demonstrating good skills in self-advocacy is to *yell* at a teacher that you'd like a seat at the front of class.
6. An example of *demonstrating* self-advocacy is when a girl tells her friend that her feelings have been hurt.
7. Sometimes people *don't do what you ask* even when the request is made in a polite way.
8. It's very *easy* to politely ask for something when you are angry.

Thumbs-Up or Thumbs-Down

Instructor reads:

1. When you apply for a job at a grocery store, you let your employer know if you need *accommodations,* such as a short sensory break every hour.

2. You find out that another girl is saying mean things about you behind your back, so you *politely confront* her about it.
3. Your mom asks you to do ten things at once. You can't keep everything straight, so you ask her to *slow down* and speak *more clearly.*
4. You go on a date and let your date know what types of sensory things—lights, noises, crowds, and types of touch—*bother* you and how you handle that.
5. You leave class to take a short break *without* telling the teacher what you're doing or where you're going.
6. You call your friends *"idiots"* after they invite you to go to an amusement park because they *should know* you don't like to go on rides.
7. You receive the wrong change from the cashier at the grocery store and start *screaming and yelling,* proclaiming you've been "robbed!"
8. Instead of calmly saying what you need in any given situation, you keep your needs quiet, sulk, and then complain that no one understands you.

Skits

Instructor reads: Practice the following skits with a classmate. Select one skit to be videotaped by your teacher for the class. Words in **bold** are meant to be read with expression. Brackets are used to give acting directions. One student in each group should read the introduction, including the plot, setting, and key concepts, for each skit before choosing actors to portray each role. Good luck!

Skit 1: Self-Advocacy in the Classroom

Students choose one person to read the introduction before choosing characters and practicing the skit.

INTRODUCTION

Plot: J.J. needs it absolutely quiet when he's taking a test, and it's usually noisy in his classroom, so he approaches his teacher, Mr. Ellingworth, to talk about it. The actors are J.J. and Mr. Ellingworth.

Setting: In Mr. Ellingworth's classroom just before school starts

56

Key concept: Talk to teachers at school if you have a problem that they can help you with.

<u>**Skit**</u>

J.J.: [Walking into the classroom] Excuse me, Mr. Ellingworth, are you busy?
Mr. Ellingworth: No, I've got some time. [Pause] What's on your mind, J.J.?
J.J.: Well, I really like your class, and I've been studying hard for the test that's coming up, but I have a little problem.
Mr. Ellingworth: **Oh really**, what is it?
J.J.: Well, this classroom gets pretty **loud** with all the students we have in here. I usually have a hard time concentrating on a test if there's any noise at all in the room. I was wondering if I could take the test either in the resource room or before or after school with you.
Mr. Ellingworth: I don't have a problem with that at all. [Pause] In fact, I'm glad you asked. When I hand out the test, take it to Room 2B. I will let Mrs. Johnson know you'll be coming down to work on it. [Smiling] Just be sure to hand the test to her when you're finished.
J.J.: [Smiling and starting to walk out of the room] Thanks, Mr. Ellingworth.
Mr. Ellingworth: **Sure thing.** [Pause] Thanks for bringing it up—I didn't even realize this was an issue for you.
End of skit

Students answer in writing: How did J.J. advocate for himself with Mr. Hall?

Skit 2: Self-Advocacy with a Friend

Students choose one person to read the introduction before choosing characters and practicing the skit.

<u>**Introduction**</u>

Plot: C.J. usually lets J.J. make all the plans. Not this time. The actors are C.J. and J.J.
Setting: At school in the hallway
Key concept: Use self-advocacy with friends as needed.

<u>**Skit**</u>

C.J.: [Smiling] Hi J.J. How's it going?
J.J.: [Smiling] Pretty good.

C.J.: Hey, [Pause] I was thinking about this upcoming weekend and wanted to know if you'd like to do something **other** than play video games at your house. [Pause] There's a new movie out that **I'd really like to see**. Do you want to go with me?

J.J.: Well, we **always** play video games on Saturday. [Pause] **I don't know.**

C.J.: Yeah, that's what **I mean**. Sometimes I would like to do something **other** than just that. [Pause] This time I'd really like to choose what we do.

J.J.: Well, I haven't been to the movies in a long time, and you do raise a good point. [Pause] In that case, sure. [Smiling] **Why not?!**

C.J.: Cool. We're on! [Leaving] See you Saturday.

J.J.: [Leaving] Yeah, see ya then. Bye.

END OF SKIT

Students answer in writing: How did C.J. ask for what he wanted in a polite way?

Skit 3: Standing Up to a Bully

Students choose one person to read the introduction before choosing characters and practicing the skit.

INTRODUCTION

Plot: A.J. has been bullying J.J., and J.J. decides to stands up to him. The actors are A.J. and J.J.

Setting: At school in the hallway

Key concept: Self-advocacy can be used with bullies.

SKIT

J.J.: Hey, A.J. [Walking up to A.J.] What's going on?

A.J.: [Standing with arms folded] Nothing, **punk. Why?**

J.J.: I just wanted to tell you that I **don't appreciate** the way you try to embarrass me in front of your friends. In fact, I'd like you to **knock it off**.

A.J.: And what if I don't? [Walks up to J.J. in his space] What are you going to do about it?

J.J.: Well, we'll just have to see. [Shrugs] But for now, I'm just asking you to stop.

A.J.: [Walking away] Whatever.

J.J.: [Leaving] Yeah, whatever then.

END OF SKIT

Students answer in writing: How did J.J. stand up to the bully?

Skit 4: Asking a Teacher to Slow Down

Students choose one person to read the introduction before choosing characters and practicing the skit.

INTRODUCTION

Plot: C.J. is having a hard time in class because the teacher is talking too fast. The actors are C.J. and Mrs. Rayski (or your actual teacher's name).
Setting: In the classroom at school; the teacher has just started class.
Key concept: Self-advocacy can be used with teachers during class.

SKIT

Mrs. Rayski: [Speaking very quickly] Good morning class. Open your books to page twenty-nine, take out a notebook, get your blue pen, write your name, and look at me when you're done.
C.J.: [Looking confused] Can you repeat that, please?
Mrs. Rayski: [Still speaking quickly] Oh, I said, open your book to page twenty-nine, take out a notebook, get your blue pen, write your name, and look at me when you're done.
C.J.: Actually, Mrs. Rayski, I meant to ask you if you'd please **slow down**. When you talk so fast, I can't understand what you want me to do.
Mrs. Rayski: OK, C.J. [Pause] I guess I didn't realize that. I would be happy to slow down.
C.J.: Thanks. [Pause] I'd appreciate it!
Mrs. Rayski: No problem. [Speaking slowly] Now please just open your book to page twenty-nine and then take out your notebook and blue pen. [Pause] After that, write your name down and look at me so I know you are finished.
C.J.: [Smiling] **Got it!**
END OF SKIT

Students answer in writing: How did C.J. ask for what he needed in a polite way?

Group Discussion

Instructor reads: Answer the following questions orally with a partner, then read the steps and design a skit to present to the class.

- When is it easy to advocate for yourself?
- When is it difficult to advocate for yourself?
- What is a good way to advocate for yourself at school with a teacher if you have a problem in class?
- What shouldn't you do or say when using self-advocacy?
- When have you stood up for someone else? What did you do?
- When has someone else stood up for you? What did that person do?
- What's the difference between complaining and advocating for yourself?

ORIGINAL SKIT

Step 1: Choose a scene in which you advocate for yourself politely. Think about different possibilities, including advocating at home, at school, in the community, or with a friend.

Step 2: Create the skit.

Step 3: Practice the skit.

Step 4: Tell the audience who the actors are, where the scene takes place, and what the skit is about. Perform the skit for the class.

Generalization

Instructor reads: It's time for interviews! First pick a partner and practice your interview script one time. I will then inform you who you will be interviewing—options include school personnel, teachers, and other students. Either I will have set up an appointment to interview someone in the building or someone will join us today to be interviewed in the room. Next, complete the interview and ask the person you talked with to rate your interviewing skills on your rating sheets.

Last, hand in your rating sheets, and we will have a quick conference about how things went.

The Interview

Student: [Walking up to the person] Excuse me. Do you have a few minutes to help me with a social skills assignment on **self-advocacy?**
Student: [If the person says **"no"**] Thank you anyway.
Student: [If the person says **"yes"**] It won't take long, and at the end I will ask you to rate me on a scale of one to five according to how well I do. I won't write anything down, by the way, so I can concentrate on what you are saying. **Let's begin.**
Student: Can you tell me of a time in which you either stood up for **yourself** or someone else stood up **for you?**
Student: Could you tell me about the **opposite** of self-advocacy? What usually happens in these situations?
Student: Why is it important to ask for what you need in a **nice way?**
Student: **Thank you.** Now please write your name on the line and rate me on a scale of one to five (one equals poor, five equals excellent), adding comments if you'd like.

Interview Rating

Student's Name ____

Person's Name: ____

Date: ______________________

1. Was I polite when I approached you? _______ (1–5)
2. Did I show that I was listening with my body (using eye contact and standing up straight?) ______ (1–5)
3. Did I use a nice speaking voice? ______ (1–5)
4. Did I make a favorable impression in general? ______ (1–5)

Total score is ______ out of a possible 20.

COMMENTS: ____

____

____

____

____

____

____

____

____

____

____

____

____

____

Bingo

Instructor reads: It's time for bingo. First I will read off a number and then call on one of you to give an answer, make a comment, or demonstrate a skill. Everyone can cross off the numbers on the bingo sheets as they are called, and you win by getting five in a row. Good luck to you all!

1. *Why* is it important to advocate for yourself?
2. Give advice on how to deal with someone who tries to get you to do something foolish just so others can laugh at you.
3. Name one accommodation you could ask for in the classroom.
4. What are some reasons why it's good to advocate for yourself?
5. *When* could you advocate for yourself?
6. *Where* could you be a self-advocate?
7. What words could you politely say to someone who is spreading rumors about you?
8. What words could you politely say to someone who is rude to you on the phone?
9. What happens when you *don't* say what you need and bury your feelings?
10. What's the difference between being a self-advocate and being an *aggressive person*?
11. *Time for a skit!* Demonstrate whining, the opposite of self-advocacy. **Plot:** Your mom says "no" when you ask to go to the movies. The actors are you and your mom.
12. *Time for a skit!* Demonstrate getting angry and making demands, the opposite of self-advocacy. **Plot:** Someone tries to steal your ice cream cone. The actors are you and the thief.
13. Demonstrate asking a teacher for more time on a test using a polite tone of voice.
14. What was your favorite skit this week and why?
15. Demonstrate good body language when standing up for yourself. What would your body be communicating in this case?

16. Give an example of how someone could be a good self-advocate at school.
17. Give an example of how someone could be a good self-advocate at home.
18. Give an example of how someone could be a good self-advocate in the community.
19. Do you know somebody who is a good self-advocate? If so, how does the person act?
20. Why is it important to be calm when being a self-advocate?
21. *Problem solving:* Blake has a problem. He's at the store waiting to check out his groceries and someone tries to budge ahead of him in line. List three ways Blake can solve his problem, including one negative and two positive solutions.
22. *Time for a skit!* Pick a partner and perform a short skit. **Plot:** Someone is treating you unkindly on the basketball court by trying to take your basketball from you. You use your skills in self-advocacy to stand up for yourself politely. The actors are you and a mean kid.
23. *Time for a skit!* Pick a partner and perform a short skit. **Plot:** You are at school, and you feel as though a teacher is treating you unfairly by taking too many points off an assignment. You went to the teacher but the teacher would not talk to you about it. Advocate for yourself by talking to the principal about it. The actors are you and the principal.
24. *Problem solving:* Jody has a problem. Whenever she tries to be a good self-advocate, she isn't successful because she just gets angry and starts yelling. List three ways Jody can solve her problem, including one negative and two positive solutions.

SKILLS REVIEW

Instructor reads on Monday: Topics to review this week include:

1. Self-Introduction
2. Conversation Skills
3. Apology "Dos and Don'ts"
4. Self-Advocacy

Monday

The plan for the instructor: Host a "show and share" time. Students bring in artifacts or photographs to share with group members, who are seated on chairs in a circle. Each student has up to five minutes to talk about his or her interest while classmates ask questions. Play a board game if there is additional time.

Tuesday

The plan for the instructor: Instruct students to make posters of the review topics. Take photographs of students completing steps of the skills. Make sure each poster includes photographs, key words, and a written guide to the steps used to complete the skill. Display posters in the classroom or around school.

Wednesday

The plan for the instructor: Instruct students to finish their posters and share them with the class. Play a board game if there is additional time.

Thursday

The plan for the instructor: Show classroom videos from the skits. Also show a short video from the Internet—YouTube, Videojug, and eHow are often good sources—on one of the review topics: Self-Introduction, Conversation Skills, Apology "Dos and Don'ts," and Self-Advocacy. Students watch the video and discuss what they liked about it and tips they learned.

Friday

The plan for the instructor: Play review bingo.

Bingo

Instructor reads: It's time for bingo. First I will read off a number and then call on one of you to give an answer, make a comment, or demonstrate a skill. Everyone can cross off the numbers on the bingo sheets as they are called, and you win by getting five in a row. Good luck to you all!

1. Tell three key points to keep in mind when making a self-introduction.
2. Tell three key points to keep in mind when having a conversation.
3. Tell three key points to keep in mind when making an apology.
4. Tell three key points to keep in mind when practicing self-advocacy.
5. What mistakes should you *avoid* when making a good self-introduction?
6. What mistakes should you *avoid* when having a conversation with someone?
7. What mistakes should you *avoid* when apologizing to someone?
8. What mistakes should you *avoid* when practicing self-advocacy?
9. Why is it good to be calm before making an apology?
10. What's the difference between "whining" and self-advocacy?
11. Why shouldn't you talk on and on only about your *own interests* during a conversation?
12. *Share your story:* Tell of a time when you introduced yourself.
13. *Share your story:* Tell of a time when you had a really good conversation.

14. *Share your story:* Tell of a time when you made a good apology.
15. *Share your story:* Tell of a time when you advocated for yourself.
16. With one other person, create a short skit about introducing yourself in two different ways: first the wrong way, then the correct way. The actors are you and a friend.
17. With another person, create a short skit about having a conversation in two different ways, based on a friend asking "What have you been up to lately?" First do it the wrong way, then do it the correct way. The actors are you and a friend.
18. With another person, create a short skit on self-advocacy when returning an item that is defective to a store. First show doing it the wrong way, then show doing it the correct way. The actors are you and the store clerk.
19. With another person, create a short skit on making an apology about being late to meet a friend for lunch. Do it two different ways—first the wrong way, then the correct way. The actors are you and a friend.
20. *Problem solving:* J.J. has a problem. Whenever he goes to a party, he just stands in the corner and waits for someone to come up and talk to him. He usually leaves the party feeling disappointed because he did not have many conversations. Name three ways J.J. could solve his problem, including one negative solution and two positive solutions.
21. *Problem solving:* Fred has a problem. Whenever he starts to introduce himself, he looks at the floor and acts like he is ignoring the person he is meeting. Name three ways Fred could solve his problem, including one negative solution and two positive solutions.
22. *Problem solving:* C.J. has a problem. His mom is mad at him for not cleaning his room right away when asked, and now he can't go to the school dance even though he really wants to go. Name three ways C.J. could deal with his problem, including one negative and two positive solutions.
23. Thinking back on the skills you learned in this unit, including making a self-introduction, having a good conversation, making an apology, and being a self-advocate, which skill interested you the most and why?
24. Thinking back on the skills you learned in this unit, including making a self-introduction, having a good conversation, making an apology, and being a self-advocate, which skill is the most difficult for you and why?

UNIT FIVE

NEGOTIATION

Instructor reads: Today's topic has to do with negotiating.

Can you think of a time when you negotiated for something? (Pause) Would anyone be willing to share what happened? (Students respond; instructors can share as well.)

When negotiating, it's good to keep in mind a few characters who can serve as either positive or negative role models.

Character #1 is "Jet the Jerk." Jet usually makes demands instead of negotiating for the things he wants and often gets angry if he can't get what he wants immediately. For example, if he wants some extra money from his mom, he says he should get some because he deserves it for simply living in her house. When this doesn't work, he feels disappointed and lashes out in anger.

What do you think of Jet's behavior? (Students respond.)

Character #2 is "Timid Timothy." Timothy doesn't like to negotiate either. He would rather keep his requests to himself and sulk when he doesn't get his way. For example, if his friend wants to go for a walk and he doesn't really want to, he goes anyway but complains about it the whole time because it's not really *what he* wanted to do.

What do you think of Timothy's behavior? (Students respond.)

Character #3 is "Mature Matt." Mature Matt is good at negotiating and at accepting the fact that he won't always get his way. For example, if a friend suggests doing something for the afternoon that he's not really interested in, he will most like likely do it anyway, knowing that next time he will get to choose what to do. He also communicates this well with others without being angry or pushy.

What do you think of Matt's behavior? (Students respond.)

In this unit we'll be talking a lot about negotiating. Through practice and self-control, anyone can become like "Mature Matt." The key is to keep working hard on the skill and never give up on yourself. Best wishes to you all!

True or False Quiz

Instructor reads:

1. People who negotiate well accept that they might not get *exactly* what they want all the time.
2. A person can negotiate *anything*.
3. Sometimes it's important to accept *"no"* for an answer when attempting to negotiate.
4. In general, other people are receptive to somebody who asks to negotiate because it indicates that the person is willing to both give and take.
5. It is *OK* for someone to get angry and yell at whomever might say, "Sorry, that's nonnegotiable."
6. An example of good skills in negotiating is asking your mom for a ride to a friend's house in *exchange* for extra work around the house.
7. Students can *never* negotiate at school.
8. Companies—and even countries—use negotiations as a way to work out differences and conflicts.

Thumbs-Up or Thumbs-Down

Instructor reads:

1. While at school, you ask to negotiate on a test by doing some extra credit work to make up points you missed. The teacher says, "No that's not possible," so you start *yelling*.
2. You find out that your parents are considering *not allowing* you to go to a concert you've been planning to attend, so you ask them why not and try to negotiate to go.

3. You make a request of your mom. She says, *"No, and that's my final answer!"* but you keep asking to do what you want over and over again anyway.
4. You go on a date, and the person you are with wants to see the same movie three times in a row. You like the movie all right but are not *that* interested in it, so you negotiate other options.
5. You want to use the family car on Saturday night. Initially, your dad says *"no,"* but then changes his mind after you negotiate.
6. Someone you are not friends with *insists* on negotiating about borrowing your game after you have already said, "No, not interested," so you walk away from him.
7. A friend of yours always wants to play video games after school, but you'd rather do something else on occasion. You don't bring it up but just *stop being friends* with that person.
8. After you try your best to negotiate with your parents, they still say "no," so you tell yourself, "That's *OK*. I may just have to wait a bit to get what I want."

Skits

Instructor reads: Practice the following skits with a classmate. Select one skit to be videotaped by your teacher for the class. Words that are in **bold** are meant to be read with expression. Brackets are used to give acting directions. One student in each group should read the introduction, including the plot, setting, and key concepts, for each skit before choosing actors to portray each role. Good luck!

Skit 1: Reacting Negatively to the Word "No" (What Not to Do)

Students choose one person to read the introduction before choosing characters and practicing the skit.

<u>Introduction</u>

Plot: C.J. asks his mom to go shopping. She is tired and says "no," and is not willing to negotiate. C.J. can't accept this and has a meltdown. The same general plot will be used in the next skit also, but with a different outcome.

Setting: In the living room at home
Key concept: If something you want is nonnegotiable, it is best just to accept this fact rather than to have a fit.

SKIT
C.J.: [Mom walks in] Oh, hi, Mom.
Mom: Hi, C.J. How was your day?
C.J.: **Great, great,** and you?
Mom: [Sighing] Well, to tell the truth, work was a nightmare today. [Pause] I'm totally **exhausted**!
C.J.: That's too bad, but did you remember you **said** you'd take me shopping sometime soon. How about tonight?
Mom: Oh, I just can't tonight. I'm sorry. [Pause] **I'm just beat.**
C.J.: How about if I make dinner and you **relax** for a while, and then we go?
Mom: I appreciate your offer, but really, it's going to have to be another night. **I am not going anywhere tonight, period!**
C.J.: [Getting very upset and yelling] That's so unfair. I hate you, and I hate this whole family!
Mom: Well, this behavior is **certainly not** going to get you what you want.
C.J.: I don't care. I never want to go shopping again, period! [Walking away and slamming the door]
END OF SKIT

Students answer in writing: What was C.J.'s reaction to the word "no?"

Skit 2: Accepting the Word "No"

Students choose one person to read the introduction before choosing characters and practicing the skit.

INTRODUCTION
Plot: Again, C.J. asks his mom to go shopping, but his mom is tired and says "no" and is not willing to negotiate. This time C.J. accepts this fact and makes the best of the situation.
Setting: In the living room at home
Key concept: If something is nonnegotiable, it is best just to accept it rather than getting angry about it.

<u>SKIT</u>

C.J.: [Mom walks in] Oh, hi, Mom.

Mom: [Sighing] Hi, C.J. How was your day?

C.J.: **Great, great,** and you?

Mom: Well, to tell the truth, work was a **nightmare** today. [Pause] I'm totally **exhausted**!

C.J.: That's too bad, but did you remember you **said** you'd take me shopping soon? Would there be any way we could go tonight?

Mom: Oh, I just can't. [Pause] **I'm sorry, but I'm beat.**

C.J.: How about if I make dinner and you **relax** for a while, and then we go?

Mom: I appreciate your offer, but really, it's going to have to be another night. **I am not going anywhere tonight, period.**

C.J.: Well, [Pause] even though I'm disappointed, I can understand what you mean. I know you're tired and that you work really, really hard.

Mom: [Smiling] Thanks for being so understanding! I'll tell you what, as soon as work slows down a bit, I promise to take you shopping the first chance I get.

C.J.: That sounds great, Mom. Now just you go and relax, and I'll start dinner.

Mom: Aw, that's so sweet!

END OF SKIT

Students answer in writing: How did C.J. react to the word "no" in this skit?

Skit 3: Negotiating with Your Friend about What to Do

Students choose one person to read the introduction before choosing characters and practicing the skit.

<u>INTRODUCTION</u>

Plot: J.J. wants to hang out with A.J. at home this weekend as usual, but A.J. negotiates to go bowling. The actors are J.J. and A.J.

Setting: In the living room

Key concept: Negotiation can be used with friends when deciding what to do.

<u>SKIT</u>

A.J.: [Walking into the classroom] Hi, J.J. How's it going?

J.J.: It's going just fine. [Pause] And you?

72

A.J.: Good, good. Say, I was thinking about this weekend and was wondering if we could do something a little different.
J.J.: [Looks shocked] **Like what?**
A.J.: **Well, I'd really like to go bowling.** I haven't been bowling in a long, long time, and it would be fun to go.
J.J.: [Speaking slowly] Well, I usually like to just do what we do every **weekend**—just hang out at home and stuff.
A.J.: We can do that, too. Hey, how about if we start out by hanging out at your house, go bowling for an hour, and then go back to your house and just relax?
J.J.: [Smiling] Well, I **guess** we could do that.
A.J.: **Great!** [Smiling] See you Saturday.
J.J.: Yeah. See ya!
END OF SKIT

Students answer in writing: How did A.J. negotiate to go bowling?

Skit 4: Negotiating a Price

Students choose one person to read the introduction before choosing characters and practicing the skit.

INTRODUCTION

Plot: C.J. wants to buy A.J.'s video game, but the price is too high, so he negotiates. The actors are C.J. and A.J.
Setting: In A.J.'s living room at home
Key concept: Sometimes it's helpful to negotiate to buy items for a reduced price.

SKIT

A.J.: [Looking happy] So are you ready to **buy** the video game I told you about? I really don't need it any more, and I think you'd like it.
C.J.: [Smiling] Yeah. I'm **totally** interested in it.
A.J.: Well, it's yours, my friend, for the mere price of sixty bucks.
C.J.: Did you just say sixty dollars? I'm afraid that's **way too much**. [Pause] I can offer you forty, though.
A.J.: Well, I was really hoping for sixty, but I would accept fifty **if I must**.
C.J.: [Pause] Actually, forty-five is the absolute highest I can go.
A.J.: Well, I was hoping to get fifty, but forty-five works for me. **Sold!**

C.J.: Thanks, now where's that game?
A.J.: [Handing it over] Here it is. Thank **you**!
C.J.: Thank you too. [Handing over the cash] This game looks awesome. Thanks!
A.J.: You're welcome. Enjoy it!
END OF SKIT

Students answer in writing: What did A.J. do to negotiate with C.J. on the price of the video game?

Group Discussion

Instructor reads: Answer the following questions orally with a partner, then read the steps and design a skit to present to the class.

- When might you negotiate? Think of at least two situations.
- What is a good way to negotiate? What should you do?
- What *shouldn't* you do or say when negotiating?
- Tell of a time when you saw someone negotiate. What did he or she do?
- What is a good way to react if you find out that what you want is "nonnegotiable"?
- When is it difficult for you to negotiate?
- What's the difference between making a demand and negotiating for something you want?

ORIGINAL SKIT

Step 1: Choose a scene in which you negotiate politely. Think about different possibilities, including negotiating with an adult, a friend, or a teacher.
Step 2: Create the skit.
Step 3: Practice the skit.
Step 4: Tell the audience who the actors are, where the scene takes place, and what the skit is about. Perform the skit for the class.

Generalization

Instructor reads: It's time for interviews! First pick a partner and practice your interview script one time. I will then inform you who you will be interviewing—options include school personnel, teachers, and other students. Either I will have set up an appointment to interview someone in the building or someone will join us today to be interviewed in the room. Next, complete the interview and ask the person you talked with to rate your interviewing skills on your rating sheets. Last, hand in your rating sheets to me, and we will have a quick conference about how things went.

The Interview

Student: [Walking up to the person] Excuse me. Do you have a few minutes to help me with a social skills assignment on **the skill of negotiation**?
Student: [If the person says **"no"**] Thank you anyway.
Student: [If the person says **"yes"**] It won't take long, and at the end I will ask you to rate me on a scale of one to five according to how well I do. I won't write anything down, by the way, so I can concentrate on what you are saying. **Let's begin.**
Student: Can you tell me of a time in which you negotiated with someone for something you wanted?
Student: How do you handle **disappointment** when you offer to negotiate with someone, and the person still says "no"?
Student: **Why** is it a good idea to know how to negotiate effectively?
Student: **Thank you.** Now please write your name on the line and rate me on a scale of one to five (one equals poor and five equals excellent), adding comments if you'd like.

Interview Rating

Student's Name ____

Person's Name: ____

Date: ____________________

1. Was I polite when I approached you? _______ (1–5)
2. Did I show that I was listening with my body (using eye contact and standing up straight?) ______ (1–5)
3. Did I use a nice speaking voice? ______ (1–5)
4. Did I make a favorable impression in general? ______ (1–5)

Total score is ______ out of a possible 20.

COMMENTS: ____

____

____

____

____

____

____

____

____

____

____

____

____

____

Bingo

Instructor reads: It's time for bingo. First I will read off a number and then call on one of you to give an answer, make a comment, or demonstrate a skill. Everyone can cross off the numbers on the bingo sheets as they are called. You win by getting five in a row. Good luck to you all!

1. Give an example of *when* you can negotiate.
2. Demonstrate what *not* to do when negotiating.
3. Demonstrate having a meltdown after someone tells you, "That's nonnegotiable." (What not to do!)
4. What words can you use to negotiate a price for an item you'd like to buy at a flea market?
5. What *shouldn't* you say when negotiating?
6. Give an example of what you could negotiate for at school.
7. Give an example of what you could negotiate for with a friend.
8. Give an example of what you could negotiate for at home.
9. Give an example of what you could negotiate for on the job.
10. Demonstrate a positive thing to say when someone says to you, "That's nonnegotiable."
11. What are two reasons why people negotiate?
12. What are two things you *can't* negotiate?
13. What is nonnegotiable to you?
14. Name one thing you'd like to negotiate for right now.
15. What is the difference between making a *demand* and *negotiating*?
16. Give an example of how countries negotiate with each other.
17. Are you a good negotiator? Why or why not?
18. What was your favorite skit in this unit and why?
19. Why is it important keep calm and not give up too soon when negotiating?
20. Do you know someone who is a good negotiator? If so, how does the person act?
21. Demonstrate good body language when you ask someone to negotiate. What would your body be communicating to people in this case?

22. *Time for a skit!* Pick a partner and perform a short skit. **Plot:** You are at a garage sale and you find something you want to buy, but the cost is fifty dollars and that's more than you have, so you negotiate. The actors are you and the person selling the item.
23. *Problem solving:* Lena has an issue. She really wants to get a dog, but her mom has always said "no" in the past. List three ways Lena can deal with the problem, including one negative and two positive solutions.
24. *Problem solving:* Trevon has a problem. Every time he tries to negotiate with his dad he ends up getting angry and then doesn't get what he wants because of his anger. List three ways Trevon can solve his problem, including one negative and two positive solutions.

UNIT SIX

TIME AND PLACE

Instructor reads: Today's topic has to do with the correct use of "time and place."

Can you think of a time when you responded well to saying or doing something at the right time and in the right place? For example, have you ever waited to talk to your mom or dad about something important until the situation was just right? (Pause) Would anyone be willing to share what happened? (Students respond; instructors can share as well.)

When thinking of "time and place," it's good to keep in mind a few characters who can serve as either positive or negative role models.

Character #1 is "Jet the Jerk." Jet has little regard for correctly using "time and place." He does what he wants at any time, in any place—no matter how inappropriate that may be. For example, he may yell inside of the library, laugh loudly in a hospital emergency room waiting area, or become rowdy and obnoxious in a calm classroom setting. He never thinks about waiting for the best time and place to either do something or ask for something. Jet doesn't care how he acts. He says he's just "being himself" even if others are bothered by his behavior.

What do you think of Jet's behavior? (Students respond.)

Character #2 is "Timid Timothy." Timothy also doesn't think about "time and place" very often. He acts out whatever he's feeling. For example, if he's at a high school basketball game and he's upset with his mother about getting only *one* snack instead of *two* like he wanted, instead of watching the game and having a good time, he mopes around in the bleachers away from the main crowd and quietly starts to cry. He also would never ask to talk to his mom in private about the issue because it never would occur to him.

What do you think of Timothy's behavior? (Students respond.)

Character #3 is "Mature Matt." Mature Matt is very good at recognizing that there is a time and place for everything. For example, before he says or does anything, he checks his environment. If everyone else is quiet where he is, he will be quiet. If, however, he's at a football game and everyone is cheering loudly, he will also raise his voice. He also knows not to offend others by saying something at the wrong time. He's very careful about what he says and does, and if he has a serious matter to talk about with someone, he asks to see that person in private.

What do you think of Matt's behavior? (Students respond.)

In this unit we'll be talking a lot about the correct use of time and place. Through practice and self-control, anyone can become like "Mature Matt." The key is to keep working hard on the skill and never give up on yourself. Best wishes to you all!

True or False Quiz

Instructor reads:

1. It is OK for a person to say or do *whatever* he or she wants in public.
2. People generally feel *embarrassed* after saying something at the wrong time or in the wrong place.
3. It's generally OK to *yell* inside of the library.
4. It's generally OK to tell *private thoughts* to family members.
5. When someone says or does something that doesn't fit the time or place, others may *stare and make comments.*
6. A *common* thing to do when making an error in time and place is to loudly yell, **"I'm sorry, I'm sorry! Geez! Come on, people!"**
7. A person's living room is considered to be *private* space.
8. Classrooms in school are considered to be *public* space.

Thumbs-Up or Thumbs-Down

Instructor reads:

1. You're at a wedding ceremony and you start *laughing* uncontrollably.
2. You're walking down the street to your car when you see a girl approach wearing a funny-looking hat. When you *get into your car* you say to your mom, "Did you see that girl's hat?! That's so weird!"
3. You're sitting by your friend in class. You loudly blurt out, *"I don't like that teacher,"* and the teacher overhears you.
4. You're sitting by your friend in science class. You tell an *inappropriate* joke, and you both start laughing hysterically.
5. You're on the *phone* at night with your close friend, and you vent about how much you don't like a certain person.
6. You're at a football game, and you stand up and yell *"You suck!"* to the other team.
7. You're sitting in the stands at a basketball game, and you *loudly* tell your friend a rumor you heard about one of your teachers.
8. Your friend *is in his garage*, and he tells you some personal information that you keep private.

Skits

Instructor reads: Practice the following skits with a classmate. Select one skit to be videotaped by your teacher for the class. Words in **bold** are meant to be read with expression. Brackets are used to give acting directions. One student in each group should read the introduction, including the plot, setting, and key concepts, for each skit before choosing actors to portray each role. Good luck!

Skit 1: Realizing You Are Telling a Joke at the Wrong Time

Students choose one person to read the introduction before choosing characters and practicing the skit.

INTRODUCTION

Plot: C.J. attempts to tell an inappropriate joke to J.J. in class, but changes his mind about doing it. The actors are C.J. and J.J.

Setting: In the science classroom

Key concept: There's a time and place to tell jokes to friends, and usually that's not in the classroom!

SKIT

J.J.: [Walking over to C.J.'s desk] Hey C.J., do you think you could help me with problem number four?

C.J.: Yeah, yeah, but just wait. [Pause] I heard this really **great joke**. [Speaking loudly] One day three **really fat, gross-looking, halfway naked people walked into a bar** ...

J.J.: [Looks alarmed] **Hey, hey!** You might want to save that one until later. People are starting to stare, and the teacher's **coming over**!

C.J.: Well, I suppose you're **right**. It can always **wait** until later.

J.J.: Yeah, that's a **good plan**.

C.J.: [Smiling] Thanks for saving me from a detention by the way!

J.J.: No problem. [Pause] Now weren't you going to help me on problem number four?

C.J.: Yes, yes. It's easy. Bring your book over and I'll show you.

J.J.: [Going to get the book] Thanks.

C.J.: No problem!

END OF SKIT

Students answer in writing: What mistake did C.J. make in the beginning of this skit?

Skit 2: Sharing Information at the Wrong Time

Students choose one person to read the introduction before choosing characters and practicing the skit.

INTRODUCTION

Plot: C.J. is at a basketball game, and he loudly tells his mom about his recent illness. The actors are C.J. and his mom.

Setting: In the stands at the basketball game

Key concept: Don't tell graphic details of an illness in public because it can be offensive to others.

<u>SKIT</u>

C.J.: [Talking excitedly] Boy, Mom, our team's **really** doing well. We might **actually** win this one!

Mom: [Nods her head] There's a good chance!

C.J.: [Speaking loudly] Hey, Mom, I almost forgot. I nearly puked today in the bathroom. I was like, **Uuuuuhhhhh! Uhhhhhhh! But nothing would come out!**

Mom: [Looking shocked] I'm **sorry to hear that C.J.**, but let's go talk about the details in private, shall we?

C.J.: [Pause] Yeah, I suppose we could do that, too.

Mom: How about if we go out in the hallway during halftime and you tell me all about it.

C.J.: Sounds good. Now, if we could just get a few more baskets going. **Come on team! You can do it!**

Mom: Go team, go!

END OF SKIT

Students answer in writing: Why did C.J.'s mom suggest that she and C.J. talk about this topic in private?

Skit 3: Spreading Rumors

Students choose one person to read the introduction before choosing characters and practicing the skit. Three characters are needed for this skit, instead of the usual two.

<u>INTRODUCTION</u>

Plot: A.J. tells C.J. a rumor that he's heard. Someone overhears this and gets angry. The actors are C.J., A.J., and a bystander named Grant.

Setting: In the lunchroom at school; C.J. and A.J. sit at one table and Grant sits at a table nearby.

Key concept: It's never a good idea to spread rumors.

<u>SKIT</u>

A.J.: [Looking around] Wow C.J., it's really packed in here. I hope we can find somewhere to sit.

C.J.: Yeah, the school should probably set up a few more empty tables. Oh, well! [Finally finding a place to sit down.]

A.J.: [Speaking loudly] I meant to tell you something. **Did you hear that Rebecca is pregnant?**
C.J.: [Whispering] Is it true?
A.J.: Yes! I heard it from a reliable source. [Speaking even more loudly] **Rebecca is really pregnant!**
Grant: [Getting angry] Hey punk, you better **shut up! Rebecca is my sister** and she is **not pregnant!** Even if she were, though, it would be **none of your business**!
A.J.: [Looking embarrassed] Sorry, I just thought …
Grant: [Still angry] Well, don't **think** next time and just **shut up**.
A.J.: [Getting up to leave] How about if we switch to a different table, C.J.?
C.J.: [Following A.J. quickly] That probably would be a good idea.
END OF SKIT

Students answer in writing: What was A.J.'s mistake in this skit?

Skit 4: Sharing Comments in Private

Students choose one person to read the introduction before choosing characters and practicing the skit.

INTRODUCTION

Plot: J.J. and C.J. are talking in private about what they don't like about school. The actors are J.J. and C.J.
Setting: In J.J.'s room at home
Key concept: It's OK to vent about things that bother you while in a private setting.

SKIT

C.J.: [Sitting down] It's **so** nice that we **finally** get a break from school isn't it? [Pause] I love long vacations!
J.J.: Yeah, I'm so sick of school. I can hardly take it anymore.
C.J.: **I'll tell you who I'm sick of … Mr. Fredricks.** He won't lay off me! He calls on me in class all the time just to bug me. He's **being such a jerk**!
J.J.: [Nodding in agreement] He's a lot better than Mrs. Anderson though. There's something wrong with **her**.
C.J.: I think so, too. [Pause] Oh well, that's life, right?
J.J.: That's right. Let's just hope we can hurry up and graduate so we can leave that place.

C.J.: [Nodding in agreement] **I'm with you, pal!** [Standing up] Now let's go get something to eat.
J.J.: [Getting up to go] Sounds good to me!
END OF SKIT

Students answer in writing: Did C.J. and J.J. have this conversation at the right time and place? Explain.

Group Discussion

Instructor reads: Answer the following questions orally with a partner, then read the steps and design a skit to present to the class.

- What does it mean, "There's a right *time* for everything"? Give an example.
- What does it mean, "There's a right place to *say* or do something"? Give an example.
- Tell of a time when you have seen someone make a mistake in time and place and either say or do something embarrassing.
- What are some things to observe in order to determine whether or not you should say or do something that may cause embarrassment?
- Give an example of topics you could talk about with your friends in private.
- Give an example of topics that are generally OK to talk about anywhere.
- What topics are never really OK to talk about in public?

ORIGINAL SKIT

Step 1: Choose a scene in which you either make a mistake in time and place—start to say or do something—but then stop yourself and wait until a later time. Think about different possibilities including at school, at a baseball game, on the school bus, or somewhere in the community.
Step 2: Create the skit.
Step 3: Practice the skit.
Step 4: Tell the audience who the actors are, where the scene takes place, and what the skit is about. Perform the skit for the class.

Generalization

Instructor reads: It's time for interviews! First pick a partner and practice your interview script one time. I will then inform you who you will be interviewing—options include school personnel, teachers, and other students. Either I will have set up an appointment to interview someone in the building or someone will join us today to be interviewed in the room. Next, complete the interview and ask the person you talked with to rate your interviewing skills on your rating sheets. Last, hand in your rating sheets to me, and we will have a quick conference about how things went.

The Interview

Student: [Walking up to the person] Excuse me. Do you have a few minutes to help me with a social skills assignment on the concept of **"There's a time and place for everything"**?

Student: [If the person says **"no"**] Thank you anyway.

Student: [If the person says **"yes"**] It won't take long, and at the end I will ask you to rate me on a scale of one to five according to how well I do. I won't write anything down, by the way, so I can concentrate on what you are saying. **Let's begin.**

Student: What does it mean that there is a time and place for everything?

Student: How do people react when someone says or does something in public that really should be kept private? Can you think of an example?

Student: Do you have any advice for me about sharing things at the correct time and place?

Student: **Thank you.** Now please write your name on the line and rate me on a scale of one to five (one equals poor and five equals excellent), adding comments if you'd like to.

Interview Rating

Student's Name ____

Person's Name: ____

Date: ____________________

1. Was I polite when I approached you? _______ (1–5)
2. Did I show that I was listening with my body (using eye contact and standing up straight?) ______ (1–5)
3. Did I use a nice speaking voice? ______ (1–5)
4. Did I make a favorable impression in general? ______ (1–5)

Total score is ______ out of a possible 20.

COMMENTS: ____

Bingo

Instructor reads: It's time for bingo. First I will read off a number and then call on one of you to give an answer, make a comment, or demonstrate a skill. Everyone can cross off the numbers on the bingo sheets as they are called, and you win by getting five in a row. Good luck to you all!

1. Give an example of a mistake in time and place.
2. Give an example of *public* space.
3. Give an example of *private* space.
4. What words could you use when asking to talk to a friend in private?
5. What *shouldn't* you do in a quiet setting such as in a library or place of worship?
6. What is acceptable to do in a noisy setting such as at a park or football game?
7. Describe the setting in a library. Why is it so quiet there?
8. Describe the setting on a school bus. Why is it noisy at times?
9. What topics are generally *OK* to talk about anywhere?
10. Why isn't it appropriate to talk about *each and every* topic in public?
11. What topics are generally not OK to talk about anywhere?
12. What topics might you talk about with a close friend in a private setting?
13. Describe two body gestures that may be inappropriate to display in public.
14. What can you do or say after saying something embarrassing in the classroom?
15. Where could you go to talk about something in private at school?
16. Who could you talk to about private issues?
17. Why do most schools have a rule against public displays of affection (PDAs)?
18. Have you ever heard anyone say something embarrassing in public? Explain.
19. Why should you be careful not to give out too much personal information over the Internet?

20. What was your favorite skit from this unit and why?
21. Demonstrate good body language when scanning your classroom to see what everyone else is doing. This will usually help you know how to act.
22. *Time for a skit!* Pick a partner and perform a short skit. **Plot:** You are with a friend at a football game, and he starts describing loudly the details of his recent doctor's appointment. You quietly tell him it's a private topic and then lead him to somewhere peaceful to talk. The actors are you and your friend.
23. *Problem solving:* Jenn has a problem. Whenever someone tells her something that should be kept private, she blurts it out to the first person she sees. List three ways Jenn can solve her problem, including one negative and two positive solutions.
24. *Problem solving:* Taro has a problem. He is always getting in trouble for being too loud in class. List three ways Taro can solve his problem, including one negative and two positive solutions.

COMMUNITY PRACTICE

Instructor Preparation for the Tour

1. Choose a restaurant to go to, make a reservation, and arrange for a tour. Explain who your group is, what they will do there, and what they hope to learn.
2. Discuss with the class what to expect at the restaurant as well as behavioral expectations (using good manners, keeping dinner table conversations appropriate, and so on).
3. If possible, watch a short video about eating out at a restaurant. (YouTube is a good resource for short videos.)
4. Use the script below to instruct the students to practice ordering a meal.
5. Designate a student leader to give the greeting upon arrival and the closing remarks on the way out.

Option for Practice Without Taking a Tour

Invite school staff whom students either don't know or don't know well to come to your room for one class. Examples of who to invite include teachers, paraprofessionals, administrators, custodians, cooks, and coaches. Explain to the guests how the class will be structured and that the goal of class is to practice social skills used when dining out. The classroom will be transformed into a mock restaurant, and students and guests will choose either to play the role of "customer" or of "server." Key phrases will be written on the board under the headings of "Customer" and "Server." For example, under "Server": "Welcome. Are you ready to order?" and under "Customer": "I'd like to order a glass of fruit juice and two cookies please." An actual light snack should be served. Upon completion of the script, the students should thank the guests for coming and clean the tables off before going to their next class. Students could then later also write follow-up cards, thanking the guests for coming.

SKIT

Server: Welcome. Are you ready to order?
Customer: I'd like a glass of fruit juice and two cookies please.
Server leaves and returns with the juice and cookies.
Server: Here you are. [Putting it down on the table by the customer] Could I get you anything else right now?
Customer: Actually, I would like a glass of water, too, please.
Server: Sure thing. I'll be right back with that.
Server leaves and returns with the water.
Server: [Putting the water down by the customer] Anything else for you today?
Customer: No, thank you. That was good. I'll just take the guest check when you get a chance.
Server leaves and returns with the guest check.
Server: Here you are. Just pay at the front register whenever you're ready.
Customer: Thanks a lot.
Server: Thank you and have a nice day!
Server leaves.
END OF SKIT

UNIT SEVEN

STRATEGIES IN FLEXIBLE THINKING

Instructor reads: Today we're going to be talking about how to become a more flexible thinker.

Can you think of a time you showed flexibility, such as when your schedule changed and you made the best of it? (Pause) Would anyone be willing to share what happened? (Students respond; instructors can share as well.)

When considering flexible thinking, it's good to keep in mind a few characters who can serve as either positive or negative role models.

Character #1 is "Jet the Jerk." Jet is not a flexible thinker at all. If one little thing goes wrong or his plans suddenly change, he freaks out. For example, if he's supposed to go with his uncle for an outing but his uncle gets sick and can't make it, Jet stomps around the house for hours yelling that it's "so unfair." Jet does not think of anyone else's feelings but his own.

What do you think of Jet's behavior? (Students respond.)

Character #2 is "Timid Timothy." Timothy often gets "stuck" in his way of thinking and whines and complains if things don't go the way he expects them to go. For example, if his schedule suddenly changes at school due to the weather, he starts to whimper and cry. He makes a big deal of even small changes in his routine and is generally seen as a whiner.

What do you think of Timothy's behavior? (Students respond.)

Character #3 is "Mature Matt." Mature Matt is OK with the idea of change. If his schedule changes, he's fine with doing something else. If something unexpected happens, he simply "goes with the flow." For example, if he was supposed to go with a friend to the movies but his friend's mom couldn't drive them there that evening, he says to himself, "No problem. We can go next week."

What do you think of Matt's behavior? (Students respond.)

In this unit we'll be talking a lot about flexible thinking. Through practice and self-control, anyone can become like "Mature Matt." The key is to keep working hard on the skill and never give up on yourself. Best wishes to you all!

True or False Quiz

Instructor reads:

1. Being a flexible thinker means *always* getting what you want.
2. People generally *like* to be around flexible thinkers more than they like to be around rigid thinkers.
3. Flexible thinkers tend to be better *problem solvers* than rigid thinkers.
4. Rigid thinkers tend to have more *disappointments* in their lives than flexible thinkers.
5. In general, it's better to be a *rigid thinker* than a flexible thinker.
6. Rigid thinking can be a *good thing* in some situations.
7. Rigid thinkers tend to have more *meltdowns* than flexible thinkers.
8. Flexible thinkers tend to have *worse relationships* with people than rigid thinkers.

Thumbs-Up or Thumbs-Down

Instructor reads:

1. You *can't* get the new video game you want so you start kicking and screaming.
2. Your schedule abruptly changes, but you have *no problem* dealing with it.
3. Your friend wants to do something other than what you want to do, so you say *"OK."*
4. Your mom says you can't go to the movies Saturday night, so you refuse to talk, lock yourself in your room, and punch a hole in the wall.

5. You *refuse* to do anything your friend wants to do.
6. You were looking forward to seeing your uncle, but he got sick at the last minute and had to cancel, so you say, *"That's OK.* We'll see each other someday."
7. You want to go to the store to buy a video game that's recently come out, but your mom says "no," so you *negotiate* and are able to get what you want.
8. You were planning to do something special in your classroom at school, but school was canceled due to bad weather, so you tell yourself, "That's fine. Today will still be fun!"

Skits

Instructor reads: Practice the following skits with a classmate. Select one skit to be videotaped by your teacher for the class. Words that are in **bold** are meant to be read with expression. Brackets are used to give acting directions. One student in each group should read the introduction, including the plot, setting, and key concepts, for each skit before choosing actors to portray each role. Good luck!

Skit 1: Using Positive Self-Talk as a Strategy to Be Flexible

Students choose one person to read the introduction before choosing characters and practicing the skit.

INTRODUCTION

Plot: As a consequence for getting a terrible report card, C.J.'s mom says he can't go to the movies on Saturday night as planned and he must stay home and complete all his missing assignments. C.J. deals with this by using positive self-talk. The actors are C.J. and Mom. This general plot will be used in the next three skits also, but with different outcomes.

Setting: In the kitchen at home

Key concept: Positive self-talk means thinking something positive to handle situations that may be disappointing. If you have a consequence, use positive self-talk to get through it.

<u>SKIT</u>

C.J.: [Walking into the kitchen] Hey Mom, can I still go to the movies on Saturday night?

Mom: You've got to be kidding me, right? After looking at your report card, you'll **be lucky** if you get out of the house within the next month! [Getting very angry] It's time to buckle down about school and not worry so much about your free-time activities.

C.J.: [Getting upset at first but then calming down by talking to himself in a positive way. C.J. says to himself in a whisper] *I can handle this. All I really have to do is get my grades up and then I'll have more free time. Maybe it won't be so bad staying home after all. After I finish up late assignments, I may even have time to watch some old movies that I like. This is going to be OK.*

Mom: [Looking worried] Are you all right? It looks like you're deep in thought.

C.J.: [Looking happy] Oh yeah, I'm fine. I was just thinking of something I can do at home **after** I finish some of my make-up work.

Mom: [Smiling] Well, I'll be darned. You're impressing me! A year ago you would have had a complete meltdown if I told you something like this. You must really be growing up.

C.J.: [Looking proud] I guess so, Mom. It was bound to happen sooner or later.

Mom: Still, I'm proud of you. Have a good day now.

C.J.: [Leaving the room] Thanks, you too.

END OF SKIT

Students answer in writing: How did C.J. make himself feel better after hearing the news that he couldn't go to the movies?

Skit 2: Using a Problem-Solving Strategy to Be Flexible

Students choose one person to read the introduction before choosing characters and practicing the skit.

<u>INTRODUCTION</u>

Plot: As a consequence for having a terrible report card, C.J.'s mom says he can't go to the movies on Saturday night as planned and must stay home and complete make-up assignments. C.J. deals with this positively by using a problem-solving approach. The actors are C.J. and Mom.

Setting: In the kitchen at home

Key concept: If you have a consequence, use your problem-solving skills to get through it.

<u>SKIT</u>

C.J.: [Walking into the kitchen] Hey, Mom, can I still go to the movies on Saturday night?

Mom: You've got to be kidding me, right? After looking at your report card, you'll **be lucky** if you get out of the house within the next month! [Getting very angry] It's time to buckle down about school and not worry so much about your free-time activities.

C.J.: [Getting angry at first but then calming down. C.J. whispers to himself] *When I think of my problem-solving abilities, I think of three ways to handle any situation. The first option is to do something negative like start yelling how unfair this is and how much I hate my life. This wouldn't be the best choice. The next option would be to stay at home and call a friend to help me feel better. The third option would be to accept the consequence and make the best of the situation by working hard and telling myself that the sooner I get my grades up, the sooner I can start doing more of what I want to do.*

Mom: [Looks worried] Are you all right? It looks like you're deep in thought.

C.J.: [Looks happy] Oh yeah, I'm fine. I was just thinking of some ways I can handle this without blowing up. I'm thinking I'll work on my homework this afternoon and then call some of my friends later for support.

Mom: [Smiling] Well, I'll be darned. You're impressing me! A year ago you would have had a complete meltdown if I told you something like this. You must really be growing up.

C.J.: [Looking proud] I guess so, Mom. It was bound to happen sooner or later.

Mom: Still, I'm proud of you. Have a good day now.

C.J.: [Leaving the room] Thanks, you too.

END OF SKIT

Students answer in writing: What positive problem-solving strategy did C.J. use?

Skit 3: Using Negotiation Skills as a Strategy to Be Flexible

Students choose one person to read the introduction before choosing characters and practicing the skit.

Introduction

Plot: As a consequence for having a terrible report card, C.J.'s mom says he can't go to the movies on Saturday night as planned and must stay home and complete make-up assignments. C.J. deals with this positively by using his negotiation skills. The actors are C.J. and Mom.
Setting: In the kitchen at home
Key concept: It's OK to ask to negotiate if you are willing to accept the word "no."

Skit

C.J.: [Walking into the kitchen] Hey, Mom, can I still go out on Saturday night?
Mom: You've got to be kidding me, right? After looking at your report card, you'll **be lucky** if you get out of the house within the next month! [Getting very angry] It's time to buckle down about school and not worry so much about your free-time activities.
C.J.: [Getting angry at first but then calming down by thinking of using negotiating] Well, you know, Mom, I've been practicing my skills in negotiation.
Mom: [Looking interested] Oh really? [Pause] I'm listening.
C.J.: Well, I was wondering if going out on Saturday night may be an issue that is negotiable, or if it is totally nonnegotiable?
Mom: [Looking thoughtfully] Actually, I had it pretty much set to be nonnegotiable, but I am willing to reconsider. What did you have in mind?
C.J.: I think that if I work hard over the next three days, I can pull up my grades in each of my classes to Cs or better. [Pause] I checked it out at school, and I'm really only failing those classes because I forgot to hand in my late assignments. My teachers said that I can still hand those assignments in for full credit. If I **do** raise my grades, you can verify this by looking at the grades on our school website. If my grades aren't Cs by Friday I'll just forget about going out and stay home to study. [Pause] How does that sound?
Mom: [Smiling] Well, I'll be darned. Let's give this a try. You're impressing me! A year ago you would have had a complete meltdown over this and wouldn't have come up with a positive alternative. You must really be growing up.
C.J.: [Looking proud] I guess so, Mom. It was bound to happen sooner or later.
Mom: Still, I'm proud of you. Have a good day now.
C.J.: [Leaving the room] Thanks, you too.
End of skit

Students answer in writing: Why might Mom have accepted C.J.'s offer to negotiate in this case?

Skit 4: Handling Disappointment

Students choose one person to read the introduction before choosing characters and practicing the skit.

INTRODUCTION

Plot: As a consequence for having a terrible report card, C.J.'s mom says he can't go to the movies on Saturday night as planned and must stay home and complete make-up assignments. C.J. deals with this positively by handling his disappointment. The actors are C.J. and Mom.
Setting: In the kitchen at home
Key concept: If you have a consequence, try to handle your disappointment by talking it out.

SKIT

A.J.: [Walking into the kitchen] Hey, Mom, can I still go out on Saturday night?
Mom: You've got to be kidding me, right? After looking at your report card, you'll **be lucky** if you get out of the house within the next month! [Getting very angry] It's time to buckle down about school and not worry so much about your free-time activities.
C.J.: [Getting angry at first but then calming down and deciding to handle his disappointment by talking it out to himself] Well, this stinks, but I guess I deserve it. I really haven't been putting much effort into school lately. [Pause] I just am feeling so overwhelmed at this time in the semester. Sometimes I feel like quitting school all together.
Mom: [Looking concerned] I'm sorry to hear you're so stressed. I didn't realize that. I just assumed you were being **difficult**.
C.J.: Well, I *am* being difficult, but I think it's because of the stress. I'm sorry, Mom.
Mom: [Looking thoughtful] Hey, how about if I stay home on Saturday night too and help you with your make-up assignments? We may both end up feeling better about all this. And, by the way, I'm impressed with the way that you handled this disappointment and then told me about what's **really** going on with you. A year ago you would have had a complete meltdown if I told you something like this. You must really be growing up.

C.J.: [Looking proud] I guess so, Mom. It was bound to happen sooner or later.
Mom: Still, I'm proud of you. Have a good day now.
C.J.: Thanks, you too.
END OF SKIT

Students answer in writing: How did C.J. deal with disappointment in this skit?

Group Discussion

Instructor reads: Answer the following questions orally with a partner, then read the steps and design a skit to present to the class.

- When is it easy to be a flexible thinker?
- When is it difficult to be a flexible thinker?
- What two things can you can say to yourself when things don't go your way?
- In general, do you tend to be a more flexible or a more rigid thinker? Explain.
- Does your reaction to disappointment depend on what kind of day you're having? Explain.
- What disappointments are especially hard for you to deal with?
- What's one thing you can do today to show flexible thinking?

ORIGINAL SKIT

Step 1: Pick a scene in which you choose to be flexible. Think about different possibilities, including situations that change at home, at school, with a friend, or with other adults. For example, you are at school and suddenly your whole schedule changes, and on top of it your teacher asks you to turn in an additional assignment. How do you respond?
Step 2: Create the skit.
Step 3: Practice the skit.
Step 4: Tell the audience who the actors are, where the scene takes place, and what the skit is about. Perform the skit for the class.

Generalization

Instructor reads: It's time for interviews! First pick a partner and practice your interview script one time. I will then inform you who you will be interviewing—options include school personnel, teachers, and other students. Either I will have set up an appointment to interview someone in the building or someone will join us today to be interviewed in the room. Next, complete the interview and ask the person you talked with to rate your interviewing skills on your rating sheets. Last, hand in your rating sheets, and we will have a quick conference about how things went.

The Interview

Student: [Walking up to the person] Excuse me. Do you have a few minutes to help me with a social skills assignment on **the importance of flexible thinking**?
Student: [If the person says **"no"**] Thank you anyway.
Student: [If the person says **"yes"**] It won't take long, and at the end I will ask you to rate me on a scale of one to five according to how well I do. I won't write anything down, by the way, so I can concentrate on what you are saying. **Let's begin.**
Student: First of all, do you know anyone who is a rigid thinker; someone who has to always get his or her **own way** or anger follows? If so, how does that person act?
Student: Do you know anyone who is a **flexible thinker**; someone who can really "go with the flow"? If so, how does that person act?
Student: Do you think it's better to be a rigid or a flexible thinker? Please explain.
Student: **Thank you.** Now please write your name on the line and rate me on a scale of one to five (one equals poor and five equals excellent), adding comments if you'd like.

Interview Rating

Student's Name ______________________________

Person's Name: ______________________________

Date: ______________

1. Was I polite when I approached you? _______ (1–5)
2. Did I show that I was listening with my body (using eye contact and standing up straight?) ______ (1–5)
3. Did I use a nice speaking voice? ______ (1–5)
4. Did I make a favorable impression in general? ______ (1–5)

Total score is ______ out of a possible 20.

COMMENTS: ______________________________

Bingo

Instructor reads: It's time for bingo. First I will read off a number and then call on one of you to give an answer, make a comment, or demonstrate a skill. Everyone can cross off the numbers on the bingo sheets as they are called, and you win by getting five in a row. Good luck to you all!

1. Give an example of flexible thinking at home.
2. Give an example of rigid thinking at home.
3. Give an example of flexible thinking at school.
4. Give an example of rigid thinking at school.
5. Give an example of flexible thinking with friends.
6. What is one positive thing you can tell yourself when your schedule changes abruptly and you don't like it?
7. What is one positive thing you can tell yourself when fun plans you have fall through?
8. What does it mean to "go with the flow"?
9. Why is it important to stay calm when plans change abruptly?
10. *Why* don't things always go according to plan?
11. Is it better to be a flexible or a rigid thinker? Explain.
12. What was your favorite skit in this unit and why?
13. What words do rigid thinkers sometimes use when things don't go their way?
14. What kinds of things do flexible thinkers say when things don't go their way?
15. How can rigid thinking lead to problems for a person?
16. *Share your story:* When were you a rigid thinker? What happened and what did you do?
17. *Where* can you practice flexible thinking?
18. When might it be a *good thing* to be a rigid thinker?
19. What kinds of disappointments are the most difficult for you to deal with?
20. What kinds of disappointments can you deal with fairly well?

21. What are the benefits of being a flexible thinker?
22. Demonstrate use of positive body language—even though it's hard—after hearing disappointing news.
23. Which two things *shouldn't* you do when reacting to an unexpected change?
24. *Time for a skit!* Pick a partner and perform a short skit. **Plot:** You are about to go see your friend who lives out of town. At the last minute your friend calls to tell you that he is sick and will have to reschedule. React positively. The actors are you and your friend.
25. *Problem solving:* Zac has a problem. He thinks he has to do the same routine every Saturday morning of playing his video game for two hours. If his mom tells him that there's a change, however—like going to the store or doing a chore—he gets very upset and has a meltdown because it was not part of the "plan." List three ways Zac can solve his problem, including one negative and two positive solutions.

UNIT EIGHT

RESPONSE TO TEASING

Instructor reads: Today's topic has to do with responding to both mean and friendly teasing.

Can you think of a time you reacted well to someone who teased you in a mean way? (Pause) Would anyone be willing to share what happened? (Students respond; instructors can share as well.)

When thinking about how to respond to negative teasing, it's good to keep in mind a few characters who can serve as either positive or negative role models.

Character #1 is "Jet the Jerk." When another person tries to tease Jet—even in a friendly way—he usually just tries to beat them up. For example, if someone says something about the color of his socks, he punches them. Jet spends a lot of time in the principal's office.

What do you think of Jet's behavior? (Students respond.)

Character #2 is "Timid Timothy." Timothy doesn't react well to any type of teasing, and when it happens, he draws a lot of attention to himself. For example, if someone makes fun of the way he dribbles a basketball, he yells at the person to "Stop!" in a loud, whiny voice, then sits down on the court and cries.

What do you think of Timothy's behavior? (Students respond.)

Character #3 is "Mature Matt." Mature Matt likes to be teased in a friendly way but does not like to be teased in a mean way. However, he has more than one way to handle negative teasing if it does happen. For example, if someone says something to him that he doesn't like, he doesn't make a big deal of it but tells the person he's not impressed or says, "Whatever." No matter what happens, he doesn't overreact, but rather, he thinks about what he's going to say and do.

What do you think of Matt's behavior? (Students respond.)

In this unit we'll be talking a lot about ways to deal with teasing. Through practice and self-control, anyone can be like "Mature Matt." The key is to keep working hard on the skill and never give up on yourself. Best wishes to you all!

True or False Quiz

Instructor reads:

1. There are generally two types of teasing: either *friendly teasing* or *mean teasing.*
2. It's *always easy* to tell the difference between friendly teasing and mean teasing.
3. The old saying "Sticks and stones can break my bones but words can never hurt me" is *true.*
4. There are certain things that are *not OK* to tease a person about.
5. Even *friendly* teasing can be annoying at times.
6. True friends don't tease in a *mean* way.
7. Adults *can help* when mean teasing bothers someone.
8. *Most people* act like bullies at one point or another.

Thumbs-Up or Thumbs-Down

Instructor reads:

1. A boy at school laughs loudly about your new short haircut, so you *punch* him.
2. A *friend* likes to call you by a funny nickname and it makes you giggle.
3. It is *helpful* to react strongly to negative teasing such as by crying or screaming.
4. It is helpful to react to negative teasing by stopping to think *before* you respond.
5. It's *OK* to say anything you want to someone—kind or unkind—as long as it's funny.

6. It's *OK* for someone to say anything they want to you—kind or unkind—as long as it's true.
7. Friendly teasing can bring people *closer* together.
8. There are some topics that a person should *never* tease about.

Skits

Instructor reads: Practice the following skits with a classmate. Select one skit to be videotaped by your teacher for the class. Words in **bold** are meant to be read with expression. Brackets are used to give acting directions. One student in each group should read the introduction, including the plot, setting, and key concepts, for each skit before choosing actors to portray each role. Good luck!

Skit 1: Friendly Teasing

Students choose one person to read the introduction before choosing characters and practicing the skit.

INTRODUCTION

Plot: A.J. is dressed all in black, and C.J. teases him about it. The two are friends and the teasing is good-natured and friendly. The actors are C.J. and A.J.
Setting: In the classroom during study hall
Key concept: Teasing can be a lot of fun!

SKIT

C.J.: [Walking over to A.J.] Hey A.J., how's it going?
A.J.: [Smiling] Pretty good, and you?
C.J.: Not bad. Hey, what's up with wearing black clothes? Are you going **Goth** on me or something?
A.J.: Goth? No, I don't think so. I just didn't have anything else to wear and thought, "Hey, this matches, so why not put it on?!"
C.J.: [Laughing] Really? I think you're going Goth. In fact, I'm going to call you **"Goth Man"** all day.
A.J.: [Laughing] That's fine by me, but I'm **not** Goth.

C.J.: Sure, **"Gothie,"** anything you say.
A.J.: [Smiling] **Oh come on!** Sometimes I get so sick of you!
C.J.: [Smiling] Yeah, and I get sick of you, too. [Pause] Now help me get my homework done, OK?
A.J.: [Rolling his eyes and smiling] Well, OK, but you're still a **pain**.
C.J.: It takes one to know one. [Smiling and moving slowly to get his books]
A.J.: **Whatever!** [Talking quickly] Now go get your books before I change my mind!
END OF SKIT

Students answer in writing: How can you tell that A.J. doesn't mind C.J.'s teasing?

Skit 2: Reacting Negatively to Mean Teasing: What Not to Do

Students choose one person to read the introduction before choosing characters and practicing the skit.

INTRODUCTION
Plot: C.J. is walking down the hall when he meets J.J., who is a bully. C.J. gets angry at him and starts to yell. The actors are C.J. and J.J. This general plot will be used in the next skit but with a different outcome.
Setting: In the hallway at school
Key concept: If you get angry at the person who is teasing you in a mean way, it may make the situation worse because sometimes all that person is looking for is your negative reaction.

SKIT
J.J.: [Yelling to C.J., who is walking down the hall toward him] Where do you think you're going, **fatty**?
C.J.: [Getting angry] I'm just trying to get to class. **Now get out of my way before I pound you.**
J.J.: [Mockingly] **Ohh! I'm so scared I could cry.** Who do you think you are, anyway? [Getting in his space] You're just a shrimp with an attitude.
C.J. [Yelling in his face] You're really starting to **tick me off. Why don't you just leave me alone?** [Walking away sulking]
J.J.: That's it, just walk away. You're probably just going to go home and cry to your **Mommy! Crybaby!** [Fake crying] **Wah, wah, wah!**

C.J.: [Yelling and crying while running away] Shut up! I hate you. You're so … so stupid!
END OF SKIT

Students answer in writing: How else could C.J. have reacted other than with a negative reaction?

Skit 3: Reacting Positively to Mean Teasing

Students choose one person to read the introduction before choosing characters and practicing the skit.

INTRODUCTION

Plot: J.J. is saying mean things to C.J. as they walk down the hall. C.J. does not get angry and therefore does not give J.J. the reaction he is looking for. The actors are C.J. and J.J.
Setting: In the hallway at school
Key concept: You don't have to get angry when others are being mean. What is important is that you keep calm and assert yourself.

SKIT

J.J.: [Yelling to C.J., who is walking down the hall toward him] Where do you think you're going, **fatty**?
C.J.: [Calmly] I'm just walking to my next class.
J.J.: [Mockingly] Why are you so weird, anyway? [Getting in his space] You're just freaky.
C.J.: [Looking ahead and remaining calm] Excuse me, I'm **trying** to get to class. Would you **please** get out of my way?
J.J.: [Looking tough] What are you going to do if I don't? Go crying to Mommy?
C.J.: [Looking calm and staring off a bit] No, not really. I've only cried a couple of times in my life and that was over something much more serious than this. [Pause] Anyway, I'm not much of a crier.
J.J.: OK. **Whatever.** [Walking away] You're not worth my time **anyway**.
C.J.: [Talking to himself quietly while walking down the hall to class] **You're** not worth my time either. Hey, it looks like we have something in common. [Pause] Who knew?
END OF SKIT

Students answer in writing: How did C.J. react when J.J. was making mean comments to him?

Skit 4: Telling Dad Not to Tease Right Now

Students choose one person to read the introduction before choosing characters and practicing the skit.

Introduction

Plot: C.J. has just woken up in the morning and is not in the mood to be teased by Dad. The actors are C.J. and Dad.
Setting: At the breakfast table at home
Key concept: If you are not in the mood to joke around, tell someone that.

Skit

Dad: [Smiling] Hey C.J. How are you doing this fine morning?
C.J.: [Looking sleepy] I wish I could just go back to **bed**.
Dad: Well, some days are just like that. [Pause] Hey, what did you do with your hair this morning? [Pause] It looks like you haven't combed it for a **week!**
C.J.: [A little angry] Dad, I just got **up**! I haven't even taken a **shower** yet.
Dad: [Teasing loudly] **Bed head, bed head!**
C.J.: [Looking serious] Dad, I usually don't mind it when you poke fun of me, but I guess I'm just not in the mood for it right now. Would you mind laying off me a little while I wake up?
Dad: [Smiling] Sure. [Pause] I'll be sure to tease you later though!
C.J.: [Smiling] Oh, I'm pretty sure you will!
End of skit

Students answer in writing: How did C.J. handle this teasing when he wasn't in the mood for it?

Group Discussion

Instructor reads: Answer the following questions orally with a partner, then read the steps and design a skit to present to the class.

- Why do you think people tease each other in a friendly or playful way?
- Why do you think people tease each other in a mean way?
- What shouldn't you do when responding to mean teasing?
- Which adult can you turn to if someone is continually mean to you?
- How does it feel when someone teases you in a friendly way? Give one example.
- Tell of a time when someone teased you in either a friendly or mean way.
- Demonstrate what you would say to someone who called you a name or said something mean to you.

ORIGINAL SKIT

Step 1: Choose a scene in which you respond appropriately to mean teasing. Think about different possibilities to respond to, including a student who calls you a name at school, an adult who puts you down, or a kid who says something mean to you in the community.
Step 2: Create the skit.
Step 3: Practice the skit.
Step 4: Tell the audience who the actors are, where the scene takes place, and what the skit is about. Perform the skit for the class.

Generalization

Instructor reads: It's time for interviews! First pick a partner and practice your interview script one time. I will then inform you who you will be interviewing—options include school personnel, teachers, and other students. Either I will have set up an appointment to interview someone in the building or someone will join us today to be interviewed in the room. Next, complete the interview and ask the person you talked with to rate your interviewing skills on your rating sheets. Last, hand in your rating sheets, and we will have a quick conference about how things went.

The Interview

Student: [Walking up to the person] Excuse me. Do you have a few minutes to help me with a social skills assignment on **responding to teasing**?
Student: [If the person says **"no"**] Thank you anyway.
Student: [If the person says **"yes"**] It won't take long, and at the end I will ask you to rate me on a scale of one to five according to how well I do. I won't write anything down, by the way, so I can concentrate on what you are saying. **Let's begin.**
Student: How can you tell when someone is teasing you in a **friendly** way?
Student: How can you tell when someone is teasing you in a **mean** way?
Student: What's a good way to respond to someone who says something mean to you?
Student: **Thank you.** Now please write your name on the line and rate me on a scale of one to five (one equals poor and five equals excellent), adding comments if you'd like to.

Interview Rating

Student's Name ____

Person's Name: ____

Date: ____________________

1. Was I polite when I approached you? ______ (1–5)
2. Did I show that I was listening with my body (using eye contact and standing up straight?) _____ (1–5)
3. Did I use a nice speaking voice? _____ (1–5)
4. Did I make a favorable impression in general? _____ (1–5)

Total score is _____ out of a possible 20.

COMMENTS: ____

____

____

____

____

____

____

____

____

____

____

____

____

____

Bingo

Instructor reads: It's time for bingo. First I will read off a number and then call on one of you to give an answer, make a comment, or demonstrate a skill. Everyone can cross off the numbers on the bingo sheets as they are called, and you win by getting five in a row. Good luck to you all!

1. Give one example of friendly teasing.
2. Give two examples of ways to respond to mean teasing.
3. Give an example of something someone might say to you when teasing you in a *fun* way.
4. Give an example of something someone might say to you when teasing you in a *mean* way.
5. What is one positive thing you can tell yourself when you hear a mean comment?
6. What are some friendly ways you can tease a friend or a sibling?
7. Why is it important to stay calm after hearing a mean comment?
8. Who can you talk to at school if someone teases you in hurtful ways?
9. What kind of teasing comments *would not* bother you?
10. What kind of teasing comments *would* bother you?
11. What was your favorite skit in this unit and why?
12. What kind of teasing is *not allowed* at school?
13. What kind of teasing is *allowed* at school?
14. Does anyone in your family tease you? If so, what does the person say or do?
15. Demonstrate good body language when someone teases you in a mean way.
16. What words could you use to politely ask someone to leave you alone?
17. What can you tease your friends about appropriately?
18. If you're not sure if someone is teasing you in a friendly or mean way, who can you talk to about it?
19. How does fun teasing make you feel?
20. What words can you use when someone says something mean to you?

21. Demonstrate good body language you can use if someone says something friendly to you.
22. What *shouldn't* you do when responding to mean comments?
23. *Time for a skit!* Pick a partner and perform a short skit. **Plot:** You are in the grocery store and someone calls you "stupid" after you break a jar of spaghetti sauce by accident. You respond appropriately without getting outwardly angry. The actors are you and another shopper.
24. *Problem solving:* Jill has a problem. Whenever she hears comments that she even *thinks* may be mean, she has a complete meltdown. List three ways Jill can solve her problem, including one negative and two positive solutions.

SKILLS REVIEW

Instructor reads on Monday: Topics to review this week include:

1. Negotiation
2. Time and Place
3. Strategies in Flexible Thinking
4. Responding to Teasing

Monday

The plan for the instructor: Host a "show and share" time. Students bring in artifacts or photographs to share with group members, who are seated on chairs in a circle. Each student has up to five minutes to talk about his or her interest while classmates ask questions. Play a board game if there is additional time.

Tuesday

The plan for the instructor: Instruct students to make posters of the review topics. Take photographs of students completing steps of the skills. Make sure each poster includes photographs, key words, and a written guide to the steps used to complete the skill. Display posters in the classroom or around school.

Wednesday

The plan for the instructor: Instruct students to finish their posters and share them with the class. Play a board game if there is additional time.

Thursday

The plan for the instructor: Show classroom videos from the skits. Also show a short video from the Internet—YouTube is often a good source—on one of the review topics: Negotiation, Time and Place, Strategies in Flexible Thinking, and Responding to Teasing. Students are to watch the video and discuss what they liked about it and tips they learned.

Friday

The plan for the instructor: Play review bingo.

Bingo

Instructor reads: It's time for bingo. First I will read off a number and call on one of you to give an answer, make a comment, or demonstrate a skill. Everyone can cross off the numbers on the bingo sheets as they are called, and you win by getting five in a row.

1. Tell the key points to keep in mind when negotiating.
2. Tell the key points to keep in mind when thinking of time and place.
3. Tell the key points to keep in mind when thinking of flexible thinking.
4. Tell the key points to keep in mind when responding to teasing.
5. What mistakes should you *avoid* when negotiating?
6. What mistakes should you *avoid* when thinking of "time and place"?
7. How can you *avoid* being a rigid thinker? What strategies can you use?
8. What mistakes should you *avoid* when responding to teasing?
9. Why is it important to be calm when negotiating?
10. What can you tell yourself if you make a mistake in "time and place" when you feel embarrassed?
11. In general, why are rigid thinkers difficult to get along with?
12. Why is it important to stay calm while responding to teasing?
13. *Share your story:* Tell of a time when you negotiated for something you wanted.
14. *Share your story:* Tell of a time when you realized that it was *not* the time and place to say or do something.

15. *Share your story:* Tell of a time when you were a flexible thinker.
16. *Share your story:* Tell of a time when you responded well to teasing.
17. *Time for a skit!* With one other person, create a short skit. **Plot:** Negotiate with your mom to be allowed to go to the school dance. First do it the wrong way by demanding your way and getting mad, then the correct way by calmly negotiating. The actors are you and Mom.
18. *Time for a skit!* With another person, create a short skit on "time and place." **Plot:** You and your friend share a laugh in the classroom during homeroom time. First do it the wrong way by laughing super loudly, then do it correctly by laughing quietly. The actors are you and your friend.
19. *Time for a skit!* With another person, create a short skit on flexible thinking. **Plot:** Your dad tells you "no" when you ask to borrow the car. First respond the wrong way by getting mad and yelling, and then the correct way by accepting the word "no." The actors are you and Dad.
20. *Time for a skit!* With another person, create a short skit on responding to mean teasing. **Plot:** A mean kid in school says that your shirt is ugly. First respond the wrong way by getting angry and yelling, then the correct way by calmly saying, "Whatever!" and walking away. The actors are you and the mean kid.
21. *Problem solving:* J.J. has a problem. J.J.'s friend always wants to do what he's interested in and not what J.J. wants to do. Tell three ways J.J. could solve his problem, including one negative solution and two positive solutions.
22. *Problem solving:* Sahara has a problem. She really wants to get a puppy, but her mom has said no. Tell three ways Sahara could work on her problem, including one negative solution and two positive solutions.
23. *Problem solving:* Anna has a problem. A kid at school keeps teasing her, and she doesn't know what to do about it. Tell three ways Anna could deal with her problem, including one negative and two positive solutions.
24. Thinking back on the skills you learned in this unit, including negotiation, time and place, strategies in flexible thinking, and response to teasing, which was your favorite skill to learn and why?

UNIT NINE

RECOVERY FROM A SOCIAL MISTAKE

Instructor reads: Today we're going to be talking about how to make a recovery after saying or doing something embarrassing in public.

Can you think of a time you made a mistake in public by saying or doing something you shouldn't have? (Pause) Would anyone be willing to share what happened? (Students respond; instructors can share as well.)

When thinking about how to act after making a social error, it's good to keep in mind a few characters who can serve as either positive or negative role models.

Character #1 is "Jet the Jerk." If Jet says or does something that embarrasses someone else, he usually acts as though he doesn't care. He says what he wants to say, when he wants to say it, regardless of others' feelings. For example, if Jet notices that someone got a really bad haircut, he comes right out and says it in front of everyone and then walks away—even though the other person looks hurt or upset by the comment.

What do you think of Jet's behavior? (Students respond.)

Character #2 is "Timid Timothy." Timothy has a habit of making the situation even worse after he says or does something embarrassing. For example, if he accidentally embarrasses a girl by calling her "too skinny" in front of her friends, he over-apologizes and tries to make up for it by saying things like, "Actually you look great. Lots of people like people whose bones stick out!"

What do you think of Timothy's behavior? (Students respond.)

Character #3 is "Mature Matt." Mature Matt accepts the fact that sometimes he is going to say or do something that embarrasses others and perhaps even himself. When this happens, he apologizes quickly and then either changes the subject or leaves the situation. For example, if he told his Spanish teacher, "Your English sounds a lot like Spanish," embarrassing her, he would apologize quickly and then make an excuse to leave such as, "Well, I should be getting to class now. See ya!"

What do you think of Matt's behavior? (Students respond.)

In this unit we'll be talking a lot about negotiating. Through practice and self-control, anyone can become like "Mature Matt." The key is to keep working hard on the skill and never give up on yourself. Best wishes to you all!

True or False Quiz

Instructor reads:

1. When making a social mistake that causes embarrassment in public, in most cases it's a *good idea* to go *on and on* about it, saying, "Sorry! Sorry! Sorry!" and causing a big scene.
2. In general, it *is* socially acceptable to comment about someone's weight.
3. In general, other than with kids, it's *not* socially acceptable to comment about someone's age.
4. It is generally not socially acceptale to make sexual comments in public.
5. When causing someone to feel embarrassed, it is a good idea to say *"sorry,"* either immediately or at a later time.
6. In some cases it's *best* to make an excuse and leave the situation after you have made a social mistake.
7. Most people have either *said* something or *done* something to unintentionally embarrass or hurt someone else's feelings.
8. When a social mistake has been made in a group, it is *common* for people to laugh, get overly talkative or overly quiet, and look tense.

Thumbs-Up or Thumbs-Down

Instructor reads:

1. You are at a sporting event sitting with all the other fans on your team's side, and you yell loudly about a mistake a player on *your team* has made.
2. You haven't seen an acquaintance in a long time. When you meet up with him again, you notice that he's gained a lot of weight, but you *don't mention it.*
3. A friend of your dad's has suddenly become bald, and you announce this fact to *everyone* at a party as soon as you see him.
4. You see an attractive girl you know. You think of saying something about how skinny she is, but then you think about it and decide *not to.*
5. You heard that your neighbor's mom got sick at work and threw up in front of everyone. When you see her, you ask her about it bluntly by saying, "I heard you *barfed* all over at work and it was really embarrassing!"
6. You notice that your classmate has broccoli stuck in his teeth. You *quietly* tell him about it before class starts so he can get it out without others noticing.
7. You accept your friend's apology after he accidentally says something that embarrasses you.
8. You say something embarrassing in front of your boss, then make an excuse to leave the room.

Skits

Instructor reads: Practice the following skits with a classmate. Select one skit to be videotaped by your teacher for the class. Words that are in **bold** are meant to be read with expression. Brackets are used to give acting directions. One student in each group should read the introduction, including the plot, setting, and key concepts, for each skit before choosing actors to portray each role. Good luck!

Skit 1: Pointing Out Acne

Students choose one person to read the introduction before choosing characters and practicing the skit.

<u>INTRODUCTION</u>

Plot: A.J. points out J.J.'s acne and ends up embarrassing him. The actors are A.J. and J.J.
Setting: In the hallway at school
Key concept: It's usually not a good idea to make comments about a person's appearance if they're not positive.

<u>SKIT</u>

J.J.: [Walking up to A.J.] Hi, A.J. How's it going?
A.J.: It's going well. [Looking at J.J.'s face] Hey, what's that on your nose? Is that a **big zit or what**? It looks like a **red volcano** or something!
J.J.: [Speaking quietly] Well, I've been trying all sorts of acne medicine and **nothing** seems to work for me. Maybe I should go to the doctor.
A.J.: Yeah, that might be a good idea. Ha, ha! [Walks away down the hall, then turns around and comes back to where J.J. is standing] Hey, J.J. I was thinking about what I said just now about your zit. I'm sorry. I shouldn't have been so **rude.** I have acne too, you know, and it bothers me a lot.
J.J.: Really? [Pause] I don't like mine much either, and I **really** don't like it being pointed out to everyone like I'm some sort of freak.
A.J.: Who would like that? I promise it won't happen again! [Pause] So we're OK then?
J.J.: Yeah, we're OK. [Pause] Do you want to do something tonight after school?
A.J.: Sure, that sounds great. [Smiling] I can make it to your place at about four o'clock.
J.J.: See ya then. [Walking away]
A.J.: Yeah, see ya! [Walking away]
END OF SKIT

Students answer in writing: What did A.J. do when he realized he'd made a mistake?

Skit 2: Pointing Out Someone's Weight

Students choose one person to read the introduction before choosing characters and practicing the skit.

INTRODUCTION

Plot: : C.J. points out A.J.'s weight and ends up embarrassing him. The actors are C.J. and A.J.
Setting: In the cafeteria at school
Key concept: It's usually *not* a good idea to make comments about a person's weight.

SKIT

C.J.: [Eating a cheeseburger] This cheeseburger is **really** good.
A.J.: Yeah. [Stuffing the cheeseburger in his mouth] I could eat a hundred of them.
C.J.: [Laughing] Well, maybe that's why you've been getting **so fat** lately.
A.J.: [Getting angry] I am not! You should watch what you say. **You're not perfect either!**
C.J.: [Pause] You know what, you're right. That was a **stupid** thing to say. I do that every once in a while without thinking. Can you forgive me?
A.J.: Oh, I suppose. [Pause] You're only human. [Smiling] At least, I think you're human!
C.J.: **Whatever!** [Pause] Hey, how's your history project going?
A.J.: Great. I'm almost done with it. Want to see it?
C.J.: [Getting up to leave] Sure.
A.J.: It's in my locker. [Getting up to leave] We can walk over there and you can check it out.
END OF SKIT

Students answer in writing: What did C.J. do when he realized he embarrassed A.J.?

Skit 3: Overly Upset in the Coffee Shop

Students choose one person to read the introduction before choosing characters and practicing the skit.

INTRODUCTION

Plot: C.J. overreacts in the coffee shop and then quickly leaves in embarrassment. The actors are C.J. and the shop owner, Sophie.

122

Setting: In the coffee shop
Key concept: If you are not happy with the food you've ordered, return it discreetly.

Skit

C.J.: [Walking up to the counter, smiling] Good morning.
Sophie: [Smiling] Good morning. [Pause] What can I get for you this morning?
C.J.: I'd like one hot cocoa and a lemon bar, please.
Sophie: [Goes to get the order] Here you are.
C.J.: [In a loud voice] Good gravy! That lemon bar looks all **rotten** and **mushy. Gross!** I don't want to eat that. **Throw it away! Throw it away!**
Sophie: [Angrily] Well, I'm sorry **you** don't like the looks of it, but I made it **fresh** today. [Pause] Our store has won several **awards** for our baked goods by the way, and I'm sure it is just fine.
C.J.: [Pauses and calms down] I'm sorry. I don't know what came over me. I'm sure it's a **perfectly good** lemon bar. Perhaps I'll just take the hot cocoa to go.
Sophie: OK, that'll be three dollars and fifty cents.
C.J.: [Giving her a five-dollar bill] Here you go. Keep the change.
Sophie: Thank you. [Still a bit angry and sarcastic] Have a nice day.
C.J.: [Running for the door] You, too.
End of skit

Students answer in writing: What could C.J. have said politely if he didn't like the lemon bar?

Skit 4: Prying into Someone Else's Business

Students choose one person to read the introduction before choosing characters and practicing the skit.

Introduction

Plot: A.J. is over at C.J.'s house, talking to his mom, Jan. He starts to ask questions that make her feel uncomfortable. The actors are A.J. and Jan.
Setting: In Jan's house
Key concept: It's not OK to pry into someone's life by asking personal questions such as about finances, marriage, or family life.

<u>**SKIT**</u>

A.J.: [Walking into the house] Hi, Jan.
Jan: Oh, hi A.J. [Smiling] How are you?
A.J.: Good. [Pause] Is C.J. around?
Jan: Not yet, but he should be home any minute now. [Pause] You're welcome to wait here for a bit if you'd like. Would you like a snack or something?
A.J.: Thanks anyway, but I think I'm OK. [Pause] By the way, I heard that your ex-husband divorced you because you were so crabby. Is that really what happened?
Jan: [Looking tense and embarrassed] Well, I don't know about that. [Pause] We had a lot of issues that we just couldn't seem to work through.
A.J.: [Looking sad] Hey, I'm sorry. I didn't mean to pry here. [Pause] I should have kept my mouth shut.
Jan: That's OK really. [Pause] It's just that it was … how should I say it? Complicated.
A.J.: I understand. That's totally your business. [Talking quickly] Say, here comes C.J. I think I'll just meet him at the door and we'll get going.
Jan: OK. See you some other time.
A.J.: [Leaving quickly] Yeah, see ya.
END OF SKIT

Students answer in writing: Why shouldn't A.J. have asked Jan about what caused her divorce?

Group Discussion

Instructor reads: Answer the following questions orally with a partner, then read the steps and design a skit to present to the class.

- How can you that tell you've embarrassed someone?
- Give an example of two topics that might embarrass someone.
- Give an example of two topics that are generally OK to talk about anywhere.
- What two conversation topics are generally *not* OK to bring up in public?
- If you make a social mistake, what can you say to change the subject?
- If you do make a social mistake, what's a good way to leave the situation?

- What can you tell *yourself* if you've embarrassed someone else by accident?
- Demonstrate how you start a conversation with a teacher at school.

<u>ORIGINAL SKIT</u>

Step 1: Choose a scene in which you make a good recovery from a social error. Think about different possibilities, including saying something embarrassing in a group, with a teacher or other adult, or with your friend.
Step 2: Create the skit.
Step 3: Practice the skit.
Step 4: Tell the audience who the actors are, where the scene takes place, and what the skit is about. Perform the skit for the class.

Generalization

Instructor reads: It's time for interviews! First pick a partner and practice your interview script one time. I will then inform you who you will be interviewing—options include school personnel, teachers, and other students. Either I will have set up an appointment to interview someone in the building or someone will join us today to be interviewed in the room. Next, complete the interview and ask the person you talked with to rate your interviewing skills on your rating sheets. Last, hand in your rating sheets, and we will have a quick conference about how things went.

The Interview

Student: [Walking up to the person] Excuse me. Do you have a few minutes to help me with a social skills assignment on **making a recovery after making a social mistake**?
Student: [If the person says **"no"**] Thank you anyway.
Student: [If the person says **"yes"**] It won't take long, and at the end I will ask you to rate me on a scale of one to five according to how well I do. **Let's begin.**
Student: Has **anyone** ever said something to you in social situation that embarrassed you? If so, what happened?

Student: Have **you** ever found yourself saying something in public that didn't go over well in a group? If so, what happened?
Student: What's a good way to handle a situation when you accidentally offend or embarrass someone in public?
Student: **Thank you.** Now please write your name on the line and rate me on a scale of one to five (one equals poor and five equals excellent), adding comments if you wish.

Interview Rating

Student's Name ______________________________

Person's Name: ______________________________

Date: ______________________

1. Was I polite when I approached you? _______ (1–5)
2. Did I show that I was listening with my body (using eye contact and standing up straight?) ______ (1–5)
3. Did I use a nice speaking voice? ______ (1–5)
4. Did I make a favorable impression in general? ______ (1–5)

Total score is ______ out of a possible 20.

COMMENTS: ______________________________

Bingo

Instructor reads: It's time for bingo. First I will read off a number and then call on one of you to give an answer, make a comment, or demonstrate a skill. Everyone can cross off the numbers on the bingo sheets as they are called, and you win by getting five in a row. Good luck to you all!

1. Why do we sometimes end up saying things that embarrass others?
2. Demonstrate how you could apologize to a friend after embarrassing him or her in front of others.
3. What should you do if you *can't decide* whether or not to say something potentially embarrassing?
4. How might someone react after feeling embarrassed in public?
5. What can you do after unintentionally embarrassing someone in a group situation?
6. How can you respond if someone says to *you*, "I'm sorry. I didn't mean to say that and embarrass you."
7. Is it normal to occasionally make a social mistake in which you say something you shouldn't have?
8. Is it *easy* or *difficult* to forgive yourself when making social mistakes?
9. What is the difference between *intentionally* and *unintentionally* embarrassing someone?
10. What topics in general might embarrass a person when said before a group?
11. How can you tell if someone is *not sorry* for embarrassing another person in public?
12. What positive words can you tell *yourself* after making a social mistake?
13. What words could you say to excuse yourself from a situation after you make a social mistake?
14. What words can you say to briefly apologize for saying something embarrassing to someone?
15. How can you tell whether or not you get *overly embarrassed* in group situations?

16. What kinds of things would embarrass you if they were pointed out about you in public?
17. What kinds of things would *not* embarrass you if they were pointed out about you in public?
18. Demonstrate polite body language and tone of voice as you say, "Hey, sorry I said that. I didn't mean to embarrass you."
19. What *shouldn't* you say or do after you make a social mistake in which you embarrass someone?
20. Imagine you just accidentally embarrassed a kid by saying that his or her shoes looked a little too expensive. Give an example of over-apologizing after this (what *not* to do).
21. Do you forgive small children who blurt out socially inappropriate comments? Explain.
22. What was your favorite skit in this unit and why?
23. *Time for a skit!* Pick a partner and perform a short skit. **Plot:** You get invited for dinner, and you accidentally offend the host by saying the food is not that great. Apologize and make an excuse to go home. The actors are you and the host.
24. *Problem solving:* Steve has a problem. Whenever he is in a group of people, he ends up saying something that embarrasses at least one other person. List three ways Steve can solve his problem, including one negative and two positive solutions.

UNIT TEN

INTERESTS: SHARING WITH OTHERS

Instructor reads: Today's topic has to do with effectively sharing interests with others.

Can you think of a time you shared your interests with someone and it went well? (Pause) Would anyone be willing to share what happened? (Students respond; instructors can share as well.)

When thinking about how to share interests with others, it's good to keep in mind a few characters who can serve as either positive or negative role models.

Character #1 is "Jet the Jerk." Jet misses the point of *sharing* interests. In fact, he doesn't share at all, but just talks on and on about whatever interests him without ever asking the person he is talking to any questions. For example, if Jet just got a new video game, he would talk about it endlessly to whomever came close by him. His style limits his ability to have good conversations because they are so one-sided that other people often get frustrated and end up walking away.

What do you think of Jet's behavior? (Students respond.)

Character #2 is "Timid Timothy." Timothy also does not generally participate in many good conversations. He usually has a very bored and unapproachable look on his face that other people interpret as a lack of interest in talking with them. The fact is that he would like to talk to others, but he either cannot think of anything to say or he sits back and gets upset that no one is coming up and talking to him.

What do you think of Timothy's behavior? (Students respond.)

Character #3 is "Mature Matt." Mature Matt has had to work on his conversation skills. He has trained himself to smile slightly, look at other people, and ask questions about others' interests. Matt knows that if he does this, he will also get the chance to talk about what interests him at some point in the conversation—he just has to be patient.

What do you think of Matt's behavior? (Students respond.)

In this unit we'll be talking about some ways to have good conversations with others. Through practice and self-control, anyone can become like "Mature Matt." The key is to keep working hard on the skill and never give up on yourself. Best wishes to you all!

True or False Quiz

Instructor reads:

1. It's *OK* to go on and on when talking with a person, even if he or she doesn't appear to be the least bit interested in the topic.
2. People who are *successful* in social situations ask questions when talking with others.
3. An indication that a person may be *bored* with the conversation is that he or she starts looking around the room and not at the person who is speaking.
4. People who are *not* interested in the topic being discussed tend to ask a lot of questions.
5. People who *are* interested in the topic being discussed typically ask a lot of questions.
6. *In general*, people who are good at having conversations talk about a variety of topics.
7. Almost everyone likes talking about what interests him- or herself.
8. It's important to *notice* when people become bored with the topic of conversation and either change the topic or politely leave.

Thumbs-Up or Thumbs-Down

Instructor reads:

1. You are at a party and as soon as you meet someone, you start talking about yourself, going *on and on and on* only about you and your interests.
2. You and a friend are interested in the same video game. Your friend doesn't have the game yet and you just got it, so you *explain in detail* what it's like. You can assume your friend wants to hear about it.
3. You like the same sport as another student in your class. When you see him, you both *talk about that sport.*
4. You just learned a lot of technical information about a computer you are interested in buying. You run into a girl from your class at the computer store. You know she is not interested in the topic, so you don't talk much about it.
5. You just got back from a camp that your friend is interested in attending next year. You invite the friend over and talk *a lot* about what it was like at camp.
6. You notice that when talking to an acquaintance about video games, he loses interest in what you are talking about so you *change the subject.*
7. You are talking with classmates, but no one asks questions about the topic you are talking about. In fact, others look bored. You stay on the same topic anyway because *you* want to talk about it.
8. You have a friend over to see your new dog. She loves dogs, so you explain things particular to your new dog in detail.

Skits

Instructor reads: Practice the following skits with a classmate. Select one skit to be videotaped by your teacher for the class. Words in **bold** are meant to be read with expression. Brackets are used to give acting directions. One student in each group should read the introduction, including the plot, setting, and key concepts, for each skit before choosing actors to portray each role. Good luck!

 132

Skit 1: Talking with Someone Who Shares Your Interests

Students choose one person to read the introduction before choosing characters and practicing the skit.

INTRODUCTION

Plot: A.J. just got a new puppy. He is excited to share the news with C.J., who also likes dogs. The actors are A.J. and C.J.
Setting: At school while on a classroom break
Key concept: It's OK to keep talking about a topic if you both share an interest in it.

SKIT

A.J.: Hi, C.J. [Smiling] How's it going?
C.J.: Pretty good! [Pause] **What's new?**
A.J.: I just got a **new puppy**, and I'm really excited about it.
C.J.: **That's cool!** [Pause] What kind did you get?
A.J.: [Talking excitedly] It's a beagle, and we got her from the shelter. She's brown, black, and white. I named her "Jessibell."
C.J.: Neat!
A.J.: Yeah. And the best part of it is that she sleeps beside me at night!
C.J.: [Looking interested] **Oh really?**
A.J.: Yeah. The only thing is that she's still a puppy and chews on everything around the house. She chewed up an old photo album already, and my mom's really mad at her. I'm not though. I just **love** her!
C.J.: Cool. [Pause] I'll have to stop by and see her some time. I'd **love** to have a beagle someday myself.
A.J.: Yeah. You **should** stop by and see her. [Pause] She's adorable!
C.J.: That sounds good. I will do that. [Pause] Well, I have to get back to my homework, but congratulations on your puppy.
A.J.: Thanks. [Pause] See ya around.
C.J.: Yeah. [Leaving] See ya!
END OF SKIT

Students answer in writing: How could A.J. tell that C.J. liked talking about the puppy?

Skit 2: Talking with Someone Who Gets Bored (What Not to Do)

Students choose one person to read the introduction before choosing characters and practicing the skit.

INTRODUCTION

Plot: J.J. is interested in cars. He is looking at a new car magazine when C.J. comes up to talk to him about getting a new kitten. J.J. is not interested, but C.J. ignores this fact and keeps talking on and on. This general plot will be used in the next skit also, but with a different outcome.
Setting: At school while on break
Key concept: Pay attention to see if the person you are talking to is also interested in your topic of conversation. If you continue to talk about something that the other person has no interest in, that person may get annoyed.

SKIT

J.J: Oh hi, C.J. [Pause] What's up?
C.J.: Not much. What's up with you?
J.J.: [Looking intently at the magazine] I'm done with all my schoolwork so I'm checking out my new *Classic Cars Magazine*. The cars in here are **totally cool**.
C.J.: [Speaking in a flat tone of voice] That's nice. [Pause] **Hey**, did you know that I got a really cute kitty yesterday? [Speaking quickly] It's an American shorthair, and we got her from the shelter.
J.J.: [Looking around the room, seemingly uninterested.] Well, I'm not much of a **cat person**, I'm more into cars. [Pause] But good for you!
C.J.: [Talking quickly] Yeah, she's brown, black, and white and really, really cute. I named her Annibell, but we call her Annie for short. Last night I took her for a walk through the park **in a stroller**, and she really liked it.
J.J.: [Starting to yawn] That's nice.
C.J.: And she doesn't shed much, but she meows a lot, especially at night.
J.J.: [Ignores C.J. and goes back to his magazine] Hmmm.
C.J.: [Talking even more quickly right in J.J.'s space] She also eats **a lot**. We feed her three cups of kitten food every day. [Pause] Oh, and two kitty treats every morning, too.
J.J: [Annoyed] Look, **if you don't mind**, I'll just get back to my magazine.
C.J.: [Sad] OK. [Pause] I didn't mean to bother you. [Getting up to leave] See ya.
J.J.: [Looking at the magazine] Yeah. **See ya.**
END OF SKIT

Students answer in writing: Why did J.J. get annoyed with C.J.?

Skit 3: Changing the Subject

Students choose one person to read the introduction before choosing characters and practicing the skit.

INTRODUCTION

Plot: J.J. is interested in cars. He is looking at a new car magazine when C.J. comes up to talk to him about getting a new kitten. J.J. is not interested, so C.J. changes the topic.
Setting: At school while on break
Key concept: Pay attention to see if the person you are talking to is interested in your topic. If not, change the topic or leave the conversation.

SKIT

J.J.: Oh hi, C.J. [Pause] What's up?
C.J.: Not much. What's up with you?
J.J.: [Looking intently at the magazine] I'm done with all my schoolwork so I'm checking out my new *Classic Cars Magazine*. The cars in here are **totally cool**.
C.J.: [Speaking in a flat tone of voice] That's nice. [Pause] **Hey**, did you know that I just got a really cute kitty yesterday? [Speaking quickly] It's an American short-hair, and we got her from the shelter.
J.J.: [Looking around the room, uninterested] Well, I'm not much of a cat **person**, I'm more into cars. [Pause] But good for you!
C.J.: [Changing the subject] Say, **what kind of cars** are you interested in?
J.J.: [Smiling] Oh, any kind really, but I **especially like** old Mustangs and Trans-Ams like the ones here. [Showing the pictures in the magazine]
C.J.: **Cool!** [Talking quickly] Well, anyway, I've got to get going, but it was nice talking with you. [Starting to leave]
J.J.: [Looking up from the magazine, smiling] Yeah. It was nice talking with you too! See ya around.
END OF SKIT

Students answer in writing: What did C.J. do when he noticed J.J. wasn't interested in the conversation about the kitten?

Skit 4: A Successful Conversation

Students choose one person to read the introduction before choosing characters and practicing the skit.

INTRODUCTION

Plot: A.J. meets J.J. at the park during spring break. Each shares a topic of interest. The actors are A.J. and J.J.
Setting: At the park
Key concept: Conversations can be fun if each person gets a chance to talk about his or her interests.

SKIT

A.J.: [Looking over and seeing J.J.] Hi, J.J.
J.J.: [Smiling] Oh hi, A.J. [Pause] What's up?
A.J.: Not much. What's up with **you**?
J.J.: Not too much either. [Pause] What are you doing over the break?
A.J.: [Talking quickly] Not a lot. I just came down here to go skateboarding. I'm **really into it**, and I just got a **new board**. [Showing J.J. the skateboard] Check it out!
J.J.: [Looking over the skateboard] It's really neat. I **like** it! I just got something new, too. [Pulling out some comic books from his backpack] I just bought these vintage comic books. Want to take a look?
A.J.: **Sure!** [Looking over the comic books]
J.J.: [Talking quickly] I got them at the Uptown Comic Shop last weekend.
A.J.: They sure are cool!
J.J.: Thanks! [Pause] Well, I see you're really into skateboarding now, so I'll let you go.
A.J.: [Turning to leave] Well, it was good talking to you.
J.J.: Good talking to you too. [Walking away] See ya around.
A.J.: [Skates off] Yeah, see ya.
END OF SKIT

Students answer in writing: Why did this conversation go well?

Group Discussion

Instructor reads: Answer the following questions orally with a partner, then read the steps and design a skit to present to the class.

- What three topics do you *really* like to talk about?
- Why is it important to take turns when having a conversation?
- Is there any one topic that you usually like to talk about best? Explain why.
- Who may also be interested in the topic you really like to talk about?
- How can you tell if someone is interested in your topic of conversation?
- How can you tell if someone is *not* interested in your topic of conversation?
- Are people always going to be interested in your topics of conversation? Explain.

<u>ORIGINAL SKIT</u>

Step 1: Choose a scene in which you have a good conversation, taking turns talking back and forth about somewhere you would like to visit. Think of different possibilities about who to talk to, including an acquaintance or friend, teacher, another adult, or a family member.
Step 2: Create the skit.
Step 3: Practice the skit.
Step 4: Tell the audience who the actors are, where the scene takes place, and what the skit is about. Perform the skit for the class.

Generalization

Instructor reads: It's time for interviews! First pick a partner and practice your interview script one time. I will then inform you who you will be interviewing—options include school personnel, teachers, and other students. Either I will have set up an appointment to interview someone in the building or someone will join us today to be interviewed in the room. Next, complete the interview and ask the person you talked with to rate your interviewing skills on your rating sheets. Last, hand in your rating sheets to me, and we will have a quick conference about how things went.

The Interview

Student: [Walking up to the person] Excuse me. Do you have a few minutes to help me with a social skills assignment on **sharing interests with others**?
Student: [If the person says **"no"**] Thank you anyway.
Student: [If the person says **"yes"**] It won't take long, and at the end I will ask you to rate me on a scale of one to five according to how well I do. I won't write anything down, by the way, so I can concentrate on what you are saying. **Let's begin.**
Student: What sorts of topics do **you** like to talk about with your friends?
Student: How can you tell if someone is **not really** all that interested in what you are talking about?
Student: What's a good way to have back-and-forth conversations so that each person gets a chance to talk?
Student: **Thank you.** Now please write your name on the line and rate me on a scale of one to five (one equals poor and five equals excellent), adding comments if you'd like to.

Interview Rating

Student's Name ______________________________

Person's Name: ______________________________

Date: ____________________

1. Was I polite when I approached you? _______ (1–5)
2. Did I show that I was listening with my body (using eye contact and standing up straight?) ______ (1–5)
3. Did I use a nice speaking voice? ______ (1–5)
4. Did I make a favorable impression in general? ______ (1–5)

Total score is ______ out of a possible 20.

COMMENTS: ______________________________

Bingo

Instructor reads: It's time for bingo. First I will read off a number and then call on one of you to give an answer, make a comment, or demonstrate a skill. Everyone can cross off the numbers on the bingo sheets as they are called, and you win by getting five in a row. Good luck to you all!

1. What *should* you do when sharing your interests with others?
2. What *shouldn't* you do when sharing your interests with others?
3. Demonstrate how you would talk about something you are interested in, making just two or three points.
4. How can you tell if someone is *not* interested in what you are talking about?
5. Show us with your body how you may look when you are listening to a boring conversation.
6. Show us with your body how you may look when you are listening to an interesting conversation.
7. Why is it important to ask questions about other people's interests?
8. What can you do if you notice that the person you are talking to is *not* interested in what you are saying?
9. *Who* might you talk with about a topic that really, really interests you?
10. When might you have a really good conversation?
11. What words might you use to excuse yourself from continuing a conversation that isn't going well?
12. What question could you ask another student to hear more about his or her interests?
13. Demonstrate how you would talk about a favorite movie by making just two or three comments about it.
14. Demonstrate how you would talk about a favorite friend or relative by making just two or three comments about him or her.
15. Demonstrate how you would talk about a favorite hobby or interest by making just two or three comments about it.
16. Why do people take turns in conversations?

17. What was your favorite skit in this unit and why?
18. Tell about two common *mistakes* people make when sharing interests.
19. When is it OK to go on and on about your topic of interest?
20. Who shares an interest that you like to talk about?
21. Who is the most interesting person you like to talk to? Explain why.
22. *Time for a skit!* Pick a partner and perform a short skit. **Plot:** Someone about your own age walks into the room, and you have a short conversation. You make the mistake of going on and on about something you are interested in without giving the other person a chance to talk. That person eventually leaves the conversation, saying, "I'm sorry. I have to get going." The actors are you and another student.
23. *Time for a skit!* Pick a partner and perform a short skit. **Plot:** You see someone you know at the movie theater. You each take turns talking about movies you like. The actors are you and the other student.
24. *Problem solving:* J.J. has a problem in that he tends to go on and on about only what interests him, so other people get bored and walk away from him. Tell us three ways J.J. could deal with his problem, including one negative and two positive solutions.

COMMUNITY PRACTICE

Instructor Preparation for the Tour

1. Choose a place to visit in the community and arrange for a tour. Explain who your group is, what they will do there, and what they hope to learn. Options include a store, a bank, a hotel, a police station, a hospital, or a local newspaper.
2. Discuss with the class what to expect to see on the tour and review behavioral expectations.
3. If possible, watch a short video to preview a place similar to the one you will be visiting. (YouTube is a good resource for short videos.)
4. Instruct the students to practice self-introductions.
5. Instruct the students to think of and practice two questions they might ask of the guide while on the tour.
6. Designate a student leader to give the greeting upon arrival and the closing remarks while on the tour.

Student Expectations During the Tour

1. When arriving, the student leader says to the guide, "Hi! We're here for the tour."
2. All students then make an introduction, starting with the student leader.

3. All students ask two questions of the guide, one question at the beginning and the other sometime throughout the tour.
4. At the end, the student leader says, "Thank you for the tour."
5. All students write thank you notes and send them to the guide.

Option for Conversational Practice Without Taking a Tour

Invite school staff members whom the students either don't know or don't know well to come to your room for one class. Examples of who to invite include teachers, paraprofessionals, administrators, custodians, cooks, and coaches. Explain to the guests how the class will be structured. Students should be seated around the room next to an empty chair. Guests will be welcomed in and asked to sit next to a student. A timer will be set for three minutes, allowing for both the student and the guest to give an introduction and share a bit about themselves. Students should be cued to bring two pictures from home or an item they like to talk about, such as a favorite game, toy, or trinket. When the timer goes off, guests will be asked to move clockwise around the room. When the students have met all the guests, the students will thank the guests for coming and sit back down in their chairs. Students then report to the class about how the conversations went and what they talked about with the guests. Last, students will write follow-up cards thanking the guests for the visit.

UNIT ELEVEN

THE IMPORTANCE OF "PLAN B"

Instructor reads: Today's topic has to do with the importance of having a back-up plan, otherwise known as a "Plan B."

Can you think of a time when things didn't go the way you had planned, but you made the best of it anyway? (Pause) Would anyone be willing to share what happened? (Students respond; instructors can share as well.)

When thinking about the importance of a "Plan B," it's good to keep in mind a few characters who can serve as either positive or negative role models.

Character #1 is "Jet the Jerk." Jet does *not* usually want to try a "Plan B" and gets angry a lot as a result of his rigid thinking. Things simply have to go his way. For example, if Jet is going to the movies and road construction on the way makes him arrive five minutes late, he becomes extremely upset and starts yelling and screaming.

What do you think of Jet's behavior? (Students respond.)

Character #2 is "Timid Timothy." Timothy also does not come up with a "Plan B" in most cases. If something doesn't go according to plan or schedule, rather than planning an alternative, he just complains about his current situation. For example, if he tries out for the basketball team and doesn't make the team, he doesn't consider joining another sport or club that he might *like just as well* but instead plays the role of the victim, saying, "I didn't make the team because everyone's out to get me! They're all a bunch of losers anyway."

What do you think of Timothy's behavior? (Students respond.)

Character #3 is "Mature Matt." Mature Matt knows that while sometimes things don't work out as he plans, he can still make the best of just about any situation. For example, if he and his friend plan to go see a particular movie at the movie theater and then discover that it isn't playing there, he'll think of alternatives such as going to a different movie or driving to a different theater. He is also grateful just for being out of the house and spending time with his friend and doesn't really care what they do as long as they are together. Matt generally doesn't get too stressed out over any changes that occur.

What do you think of Matt's behavior? (Students respond.)

In this unit we'll be talking a lot about the importance of having a "Plan B." Through practice and self-control, anyone can become like "Mature Matt." The key is to keep working hard on the skill and never give up on yourself. Best wishes to you all!

True or False Quiz

Instructor reads:

1. When things don't work out according to the original plan, it is socially acceptable to throw a *fit*.
2. A *good way* to deal with plans that abruptly change is to say to yourself, "I can't do that, but I can do something else instead."
3. Having a *"Plan B"* means you have more than one way of dealing with disappointments or unexpected changes that occur.
4. People who are good at coming up with a "Plan B" are *easy* to be around because they can quickly change their minds as needed and "go with the flow."
5. It is good to get stuck on just one way of thinking without a "Plan B."
6. Plan B" means your "Plan A" fell through, and now you have to think of alternatives.
7. People who find many solutions to problems tend to be *more stressed* than those who get stuck on only one way of thinking.
8. A person should come up with a "Plan B" when things change in order to avoid stress.

Thumbs-Up or Thumbs-Down

Instructor reads:

1. Someone you know starts *yelling* on the phone at a friend who says they can't meet as planned because his car has broken down.
2. You didn't get a good grade on your final exam like you thought you would. You know you should have studied harder, but you end up yelling at the teacher, calling his grading policies *unfair.*
3. You think of *additional ways* to make money after you realize your allowance isn't enough to buy that phone you want.
4. You are not picked to be on the starting basketball team like you planned. You say nothing to anyone and instead *sulk* in your room for two days, refusing to come out.
5. Someone you would have liked to be friends with is not returning your calls. You decide that she really is not interested in doing things with you, and say to yourself, "*That's OK.* I'll call someone else."
6. You really wanted to go to the basketball game tonight, but your dad said "no." You say to yourself, "It could be worse," and watch a movie instead.
7. You find out that you did not get the summer job you applied for. You tell yourself that you are no good and decide to not even try to find another job.
8. Your schedule at school changes, but you use a "Plan B" and go with the flow.

Skits

Instructor reads: Practice the following skits with a classmate. Select one skit to be videotaped by your teacher for the class. Words in **bold** are meant to be read with expression. Brackets are used to give acting directions. One student in each group should read the introduction, including the plot, setting, and key concepts, for each skit before choosing actors to portray each role. Good luck!

Skit 1: Plans That Don't Work Out

Students choose one person to read the introduction before choosing characters and practicing the skit.

INTRODUCTION

Plot: A.J. has asked J.J to go with him for the weekend to the waterpark. On Friday, A.J.'s plans fall through and neither of them can go.
Setting: In the hallway at school
Key concept: Sometimes unexpected things happen and when they do, it's important to have a "Plan B."

SKIT

J.J.: [Walking up to A.J.] Hi, A.J. How's it going?
A.J.: Great! [Talking quickly] **I'm so excited to go with you tomorrow to the waterpark.** I have everything ready—my suit, my overnight bag, some extra money. **I am ready to go!**
J.J.: [Hesitantly] Well, about the waterpark. [Pause] I don't think it's going to work out for this weekend after all. My parents just told me that they both have to work all weekend and will have to reschedule. I'm **so sorry**!
A.J.: Bummer! [Pause] So basically neither one of us is going, right?
J.J.: Pretty much.
A.J.: Well, I was really looking forward to it, and I bet you were, too. [Pause] Let's see, we can't do that, but what **can** we do? What's our "Plan B?"
J.J.: Well, you could come over and spend the night at my house tomorrow if you want. I don't have a waterpark, but I **do** have a heated pool.
A.J.: That "Plan B" sounds great. [Leaving] See you tomorrow then?
J.J.: Yeah. [Leaving] See you tomorrow!
END OF SKIT

Students answer in writing: How did A.J. handle his disappointment over not going to the waterpark?

Skit 2: Reacting Poorly to Change (What Not to Do)

Students choose one person to read the introduction before choosing characters and practicing the skit.

INTRODUCTION

Plot: C.J. reacts poorly when Mom tells him about a change of plans. The actors are C.J. and Mom. This general plot will be used in the next skit, but with a different outcome.
Setting: In the kitchen; Mom is making soup.
Key concept: When you don't have a "Plan B," abrupt changes can be very difficult to deal with.

SKIT

C.J.: [Walking into the kitchen] Hi, Mom.
Mom: Oh hi, C.J.! [Looking up from the stove] How are you doing today?
C.J.: Good, good. [Talking quickly] I'm really **excited** about going to that movie tonight. It should be a good one.
Mom: Oh, honey is that tonight? [Dropping her soup spoon] **I totally forgot about it** and made plans for us all to go to the neighborhood picnic and block party. I'm sorry. [Pause] We'll just have to go tomorrow night instead.
C.J.: [Speaking angrily] **What?** I can't go to the movies but I'm supposed to go to **a stupid picnic? You're kidding me, right?** Well, I am **not going**, and you are just the **worst mother ever**!
Mom: [Speaking loudly] That's **no way** to talk to me. You'll have to spend some time in your room now to take a break and I will have to reconsider even allowing you to go to the movie tomorrow.
C.J.: [Speaking loudly] Whatever! [Starting to leave the room] I don't even want to go to the stupid movie anyway! You ruined everything!
Mom: [Angrily] OK then, it's settled. [Pause] No movie at all.
C.J.: Fine! [Slamming the door]
END OF SKIT

Students answer in writing: How did C.J. react to a change of plans?

Skit 3: Handling Not Being Able to Go to the Movies Tonight in a Better Way

Students choose one person to read the introduction before choosing characters and practicing the skit.

INTRODUCTION

Plot: C.J. handles it well when Mom tells him about a change of plans. The actors are C.J. and Mom.
Setting: In the kitchen; Mom is making soup.
Key concept: Having a "Plan B" can help you deal with changes that occur.

SKIT

C.J.: [Walking into the kitchen] Hi, Mom.
Mom: Oh hi, C.J.! [Looking up from the stove] How are you doing today?
C.J.: Good, good. [Talking quickly] I'm really **excited** about going to that movie tonight. It should be a good one.
Mom: Oh, honey is that tonight? [Dropping her soup spoon] **I totally forgot about it** and made plans for us to go to the neighborhood picnic and block party. I'm sorry. [Pause] We'll just have to go tomorrow night instead.
C.J.: [Breathing deeply] Really, Mom? I was looking forward to the movie so much, and you know how I feel about neighborhood parties. There's no one my own age to hang out with.
Mom: You're right. You **are** one of the oldest kids on the block.
C.J.: [Talking to himself quietly] *I can handle this. It's not the end of the world! I can go to the movies tomorrow.*
Mom: What did you just say?
C.J.: I said that I can handle not going to the movies until tomorrow night. That's OK, I'll live! [Pause] But Mom, how about if I skip the neighborhood party and clean my room instead?
Mom: [Looking shocked] Clean your room? Are you **serious**? [Pause] Well, I can't pass that one up! That sounds great.
C.J.: Thanks, Mom. You and Dad go and have a good time [Whispering] with the old people!
Mom: C.J.! [Smiling] Hey, I heard that!
END OF SKIT

Students answer in writing: How did C.J. respond in a positive way to the change of plans?

Skit 4: Not Making the Team

Students choose one person to read the introduction before choosing characters and practicing the skit.

Introduction

Plot: A.J. just got home from school. He tells his dad he didn't make the basketball team and he's disappointed. The actors are A.J. and Dad.
Setting: In the living room at home
Key concept: It's good to have a "Plan B" when dealing with disappointment.

Skit

A.J.: [Walking in, looking sad.] Hi, Dad.
Dad: Oh, hi, A.J. [Pause] What's up? You look upset.
A.J.: [Talking slowly] What's there to be so **happy** about? I just found out that I didn't make the basketball team and all my friends did. **Everything sucks!**
Dad: [Looking concerned] **That's too bad.** I know that was something you were really looking forward to. But you know what? Those things happen. It doesn't mean that there's anything wrong with you or your abilities. The coaches probably had a lot of players to choose from and had to make some hard decisions. There will always be disappointments like this in life, son. The important thing is how you're going to handle this right now.
A.J.: [Looking up] What do you mean by that?
Dad: Well, there are a couple of routes you could go. [Pause] You could get mad at the coaches, or you might even think it was something personal—like you're somehow not good enough as a person. Or you could go the "Plan B" route, in which case you accept the outcome—not making the team—and perhaps get interested in something else.
A.J.: Right now I feel lousy and just don't want to do anything.
Dad: [Speaking kindly] That's completely understandable. Give yourself some time. I have faith that you will make some good decisions here.
A.J.: Well, thanks, Dad. I guess it could be worse. Maybe there is something else I'd like to do with my time now that **I have some**!
Dad: [Smiling] That's the right attitude. [Pause] **Way to go!**

A.J.: For now, I think I'll just hang out and watch a movie.
Dad: Can I watch it with you?
A.J.: Sure, why not? [Pause] Just make sure it's not one about basketball!
Dad: No problem! I'll make the popcorn and you pick out the movie.
A.J.: Sounds good!
END OF SKIT

Students answer in writing: How did A.J.'s dad help him handle his disappointment over not making the basketball team?

Group Discussion

Instructor reads: Answer the following questions orally with a partner, then read the steps and design a skit to present to the class.

- What does having a "Plan B" mean to you?
- How do you handle disappointments in general?
- Tell of a time you got angry after being disappointed.
- What are two *good* ways to handle disappointing situations?
- What words can you tell *yourself* when things don't go as planned?
- Do you think it's possible for things to always go as planned? Explain.
- What are some possible situations in which you can use "Plan B" in the future?

ORIGINAL SKIT

Step 1: Choose a situation in which something doesn't go your way. Next, tell your actor "mom" about it and come up with "Plan B." Think about different possibilities including feeling disappointed over a change in schedules, a change of plans, not getting to do something you wanted, or not getting to have something you wanted.
Step 2: Create the skit.
Step 3: Practice the skit.
Step 4: Tell the audience who the actors are, where the scene takes place, and what the skit is about. Perform the skit for the class.

Generalization

Instructor reads: It's time for interviews! First pick a partner and practice your interview script one time. I will then inform you who you will be interviewing—options include school personnel, teachers, and other students. Either I will have set up an appointment to interview someone in the building or someone will join us today to be interviewed in the room. Next, complete the interview and ask the person you talked with to rate your interviewing skills on your rating sheets. Last, hand in your rating sheets, and we will have a quick conference about how things went.

The Interview

Student: [Walking up to the person] Excuse me. Do you have a few minutes to help me with a social skills assignment on **the importance of having a "Plan B"**?
Student: [If the person says **"no"**] Thank you anyway.
Student: [If the person says **"yes"**] It won't take long, and at the end I will ask you to rate me on a scale of one to five according to how well I do. **Let's begin.**
Student: Do things always go as planned for you? If not, can you give me an example of what sorts of unplanned things may happen?
Student: How do you handle disappointment when things don't go your way?
Student: Do you ever use a "Plan B" to deal with the "unexpected"? If so, how?
Student: **Thank you.** Now please write your name on the line and rate me on a scale of one to five (one equals poor and five equals excellent), adding comments if you wish.

Interview Rating

Student's Name ______________________________

Person's Name: ______________________________

Date: ______________

1. Was I polite when I approached you? ______ (1–5)
2. Did I show that I was listening with my body (using eye contact and standing up straight?) ______ (1–5)
3. Did I use a nice speaking voice? ______ (1–5)
4. Did I make a favorable impression in general? ______ (1–5)

Total score is ______ out of a possible 20.

COMMENTS: ______________________________

Bingo

Instructor reads: It's time for bingo. First I will read off a number and then call on one of you to give an answer, make a comment, or demonstrate a skill. Everyone can cross off the numbers on the bingo sheets as they are called, and you win by getting five in a row. Good luck to you all!

1. Give an example of using "Plan B" at school after your schedule changes unexpectedly and you can't go out to lunch as planned.
2. Give an example of using "Plan B" when plans fall through with a friend who was supposed to pick you up for an overnight stay.
3. Give an example of using "Plan B" when your parents don't allow you to go to the movies this weekend as planned.
4. Give an example of using "Plan B" when you need to get somewhere and your car breaks down.
5. What is one positive thing you could say to *yourself* after hearing that you can't go to your favorite mall until your grades improve?
6. What is one positive thing you could tell *yourself* after finding out that you didn't get invited to hang out with friends on Saturday night?
7. *Share your story:* Tell of a time when you used "Plan B" after learning about a change of plans.
8. *Share your story:* Tell of a time when you didn't use "Plan B" and had a meltdown after learning about a change.
9. Why is it a good idea to have a "Plan B" in mind for when things don't go as planned?
10. What is something negative that might happen when you don't have a "Plan B" and your plans fall through?
11. What could you do if the movie you were planning to see tonight is no longer playing in the movie theater and you've driven all the way there?
12. Demonstrate having a meltdown over not being able to go to the arcade as planned (the wrong way to handle things).
13. What positive thing can you tell yourself when someone you "like" has turned you down for a date on Saturday night?

14. Demonstrate your body language when you find out you can't get the present you wanted until next year.
15. Is your family good at coming up with "Plan Bs" in general? Explain.
16. What was your favorite skit in this unit and why?
17. Tell us about one person you know who is good at using "Plan B." How does the person act when things don't go according to plan?
18. Why don't more people use "Plan B" instead of getting upset over things they have no control over?
19. What was one major disappointment you've had in your life? How did you handle it?
20. Can friends help you come up with a "Plan B" when your plans change? Explain.
21. *Problem solving:* Tyler has a problem. He wants to buy a new video game. He goes to the store to buy one, but they are all sold out. List three ways Tyler could deal with this situation, including one negative way and two positive "Plan Bs."
22. *Problem solving:* Mikayla has a problem. She has a set schedule at school and is really looking forward to going to art class today so she can finish her project that is due this week. When she gets to school, she learns that due to a special assembly in the gym, there will be no art class today. List three ways Mikayla can deal with this situation, including one negative way and two positive "Plan Bs."
23. *Time for a skit!* Pick a partner and perform a short skit. **Plot:** Your friend has just called to tell you that he can't drive you to the Vikings' game as planned because he's sick. Handle this positively using "Plan B." The actors are you and your friend.
24. *Time for a skit!* Pick a partner and perform a skit. **Plot:** You are just leaving with a friend to go to an awesome concert when you discover you've locked your keys in your car. Handle this positively using "Plan B." The actors are you and your friend.

UNIT TWELVE

NONVERBAL COMMUNICATION

Instructor reads: Today's topic has to do with nonverbal communication. Nonverbal communication means the messages we send to each other through our body language (our actions, facial expressions, and body posture) without the use of words.

Can you think of any ways you have displayed positive body language, for example, when meeting someone for the first time? (Pause) Would anyone be willing to share what happened? (Students respond; instructors can share as well.)

When thinking about the use of body language, it's good to keep in mind a few characters who can serve as either positive or negative role models.

Character #1 is "Jet the Jerk." Jet does not care what his body language is communicating to others. If he is upset, his face and body look tense and upset; if he is happy, he looks happy; if he doesn't care what is going on at the moment, he slouches and looks bored. The problem is that sometimes his body language does not fit the social situation. For example, if a friend tells him about a new video game that he bought and is excited about, he may roll his eyes and look away because he is bored.

What do you think of Jet's behavior and how his friend might feel? (Students respond.)

Character #2 is "Timid Timothy." Timothy usually has one and only one way of expressing nonverbal communication: looking bored or depressed. Most often his shoulders are slumped and he's looking at the floor or at the wall. As a result, he comes across as either being terribly uninterested in whatever is going on or is being said, even if he's not feeling that way.

What do you think of Timothy's behavior and what others think of him? (Students respond.)

Character #3 is "Mature Matt." Mature Matt knows that sometimes he has to make his body look a certain way to fit the situation in order to avoid making others feel uncomfortable. For example, say that on his way to his friend's house he just found out from his mom that the video game he's been waiting on for days has been delayed in shipping. Instead of being upset and angry while at his friend's house, he tries not to think about it and concentrates on what his friend wants to do for the day. He keeps his body language positive and attentive. He looks at the person who is talking, nods his heads slightly, and smiles a bit to show that he is interested in what the speaker is saying and is truly listening.

What do you think of Matt's behavior and how his friend might feel? (Students respond.)

In this unit we'll be talking a lot about nonverbal communication. Through practice and self-control, anyone can become like "Mature Matt." The key is to keep working hard on the skill and never give up on yourself. Best wishes to you all!

True or False Quiz

Instructor reads:

1. Nonverbal communication is *very important* to communicating in general.
2. People who smile a lot often make *others* smile.
3. No one can *tell* another person is sad unless the person says out loud, "Today I am sad."
4. Body language is another *language* like French or German.
5. People who appear angry often look tense and may *frown* or clench their fists.
6. People are often *unaware* of what their body language is communicating.
7. People generally go out of their way to talk to others who appear *angry* or anxious.
8. People who feel *happy* often show it by the expression on their face or how they walk.

Thumbs-Up or Thumbs-Down

Instructor reads:

1. A friend has a *sad* look on her face, so you walk over and ask how she is doing.
2. Acquaintances often say "hi" to you if you *usually* look angry or upset.
3. It is common to look *shocked* when you hear startling news.
4. It is common to laugh when you're sad.
5. *Talking* is a form of nonverbal communication.
6. *Smiling* is a form of nonverbal communication.
7. *Yawning loudly* in class is a form of nonverbal communication.
8. How you walk is a form of nonverbal communication.

Skits

Instructor reads: Practice the following skits with a classmate. Select one skit to be videotaped by your teacher for the class. Words in **bold** are meant to be read with expression. Brackets are used to give acting directions. One student in each group should read the introduction, including the plot, setting, and key concepts, for each skit before choosing actors to portray each role. Good luck!

Skit 1: Looking Sad

Students choose one person to read the introduction before choosing characters and practicing the skit.

INTRODUCTION

Plot: J.J. is sitting all alone in the hallway feeling sad. His body is slouched over, and A.J. can tell that something is wrong, so he walks over. The actors are J.J. and A.J.

Setting: In an empty hallway at school

Key concept: Nonverbal communication can be a powerful indicator of how you're feeling.

SKIT

J.J.: [Sitting alone in the hallway, staring down at the floor as A.J. approaches] Oh, [Pause] hi, A.J.

A.J.: [Crouching down] Hi! [Pause, looking concerned] Hey, how's it going? Is something **wrong**?

J.J.: [Staring off] Not really. [Looking sad] I guess I'm just having **a bad day**.

A.J.: [Sitting down next to J.J. and talking softly] Do you want to **talk** about it?

J.J.: Well, lately **everything** seems to be going **wrong**. I'm handing in my homework late and my grades are slipping. My parents are mad at me a lot at home, and one of my friends stopped hanging out with me **for no reason at all**.

A.J.: [Empathetically] Well, that's too bad. [Pause] I understand why you'd be upset with all that going on.

J.J.: [Nodding his head] Yeah. It's all just too much right now.

A.J.: Is there anything I can do to help?

J.J.: Well, how's your math? [Pause] I'm getting a D minus and I could use some help, I guess.

A.J.: I'm **awesome** at math. It's my best subject. Do you want to get together sometime after school and work on it?

J.J.: That would be **great**. [Smiling] Thank you **so much**!

A.J.: Hey, no problem. [Starting to leave] Just give me a call when you're free, and we'll get right on it.

J.J.: Hey, thanks again.

A.J.: [Walking away] No problem. Glad I could help

END OF SKIT

Students answer in writing: How could A.J. tell by J.J.'s body language that something was bothering him?

Skit 2: Refusing to Communicate with Words When Words Might Help (What Not to Do)

Students choose one person to read the introduction before choosing characters and practicing the skit.

INTRODUCTION

Plot: : C.J. is letting his dad know with his body language and tone of voice that he is upset about something, but he won't use words to express it, so his dad is

confused about what might be wrong. The actors are C.J. and Dad. This general plot is the same in the next skit also, but with a different outcome.
Setting: At home
Key concept: While nonverbal communication lets people know that you are feeling a certain way, communicating with words can also help to express those feelings in a way that others can understand.

Skit

Dad: Hi C.J. [Smiling] How are you doing today?
C.J.: [Saying nothing, stone-faced]
Dad: Hey there now, [walking over closer] I asked how you're doing today. **Is everything OK?**
[C.J. turns his back in anger, about to cry]
Dad: OK. Now I know something's definitely wrong. [Pause] Can you tell me about it so I can help you work it out?
C.J.: [Yelling] **No! Never!** It never works to talk anyway, so **why bother**? I know you just want to keep all your stupid money anyway! [Storms off]
Dad: **C.J.!** [Talking loudly] **What's going on?** I don't know what you're **talking about**! What's this about money? [Shrugging his shoulders] I just don't get it.
C.J.: [Yells from a distance] And you **never will**!
Dad: [Standing there looking confused].
End of skit

Students answer in writing: Why *couldn't* C.J.'s dad tell what was wrong just by the way C.J. was acting?

Skit 3: Good Communication

Students choose one person to read the introduction before choosing characters and practicing the skit.

Introduction

Plot: C.J. is letting his dad know that he is upset about something by his body language and tone of voice. This time he explains his feelings. The actors are C.J. and Dad.
Setting: At home
Key concept: It's good to talk things out when you're upset.

SKIT

Dad: Hi C.J. [Smiling] How are you doing today?

C.J.: To tell you the truth, not so great!

Dad: [Looking concerned] Hey, **what's wrong**?

C.J.: [Pause] Well, it's kind of hard to talk about.

Dad: Can you give it a **try**?

C.J.: [Speaking slowly] Well, it's just that I got my allowance, and it was only five dollars. [Pause] I thought it would be ten dollars because of all that **extra** yard work I did this week.

Dad: Oh my gosh! [Looking surprised] The yard work! **I totally forgot about that!** Yes, I **do** owe you an extra five dollars.

C.J.: [Smiling] So it was just a mistake then?

Dad: Yeah. [Pause] And I'm really sorry about that.

C.J.: [Happy] **No problem.** But can I get that five dollars now please?

Dad: Sure son, no problem. [Handing over the cash] Here you go.

C.J.: Thanks, Dad!

Dad: No, thank **you** for reminding me about it. [Pause] I would have felt just terrible if I hadn't given you what I owed you!

C.J.: [Smiling] You can always count on **me** to tell you if you owe me money.

Dad: [Smiling] Yes, I suppose I can!

END OF SKIT

Students answer in writing: How does C.J. solve his problem in this skit?

Skit 4: Looking Approachable

Students choose one person to read the introduction before choosing characters and practicing the skit.

INTRODUCTION

Plot: J.J. is sitting quietly on the bench smiling, when A.J. comes over and starts talking to him about basketball. The actors are J.J. and A.J.

Setting: At the community center

Key concept: If you look friendly, people may approach you.

SKIT

A.J.: [Walking over to the bench to sit down] Hi. Do you mind if I sit here, too?

J.J.: [Smiling and leaning back] No, not at all. How's it going?
A.J.: [Wiping sweat from his brow] Good, good. I'm getting **tired** out though. [Pulling out his water bottle and taking a drink] I'm glad I brought my water bottle!
J.J.: Yeah. [Looking at J.J. and then on the basketball court] I saw you out there. You were running **pretty hard**.
A.J.: [Smiling] Well, I'm not a great ball player, but at least I'm fast. [Pause] Do you play?
J.J.: [Smiling] I play some. [Pause] I'm not very good at it, but I **like** to play.
A.J.: Hey, want to take some shots **with me**?
J.J.: Yeah, that sounds great. [Pause] I'm A.J. by the way.
A.J.: And I'm J.J. [Smiling] Good to meet you.
J.J.: It's nice to meet you, too.
A.J.: [Getting up to play ball] Now let's go see what we can do.
J.J.: [Getting up too] Sounds **great**!
END OF SKIT

Students answer in writing: What made it made it seem like A.J. was willing to meet someone new?

Group Discussion

Instructor reads: Answer the following questions orally with a partner, then read the steps and design a skit to present to the class.

- Demonstrate how you can express any *two feelings*—for example, happy and sad—without words.
- How would your body look if you wanted to show someone you were *listening*?
- How would your body look if you wanted to show someone you were *angry*?
- How would your body look if you wanted to show someone you were *friendly* and *approachable*?
- How would your body look if you wanted to communicate to someone that you wanted to be alone?

- Do people generally approach others who appear angry? Why or why not?
- What might your body language be telling people right now?

Original Skit

Step 1: Pick a partner and choose a scene in which you act out two emotions without using words. For example, one character would act angry by pouting and stomping around the room. The other character would portray the feeling of being sad and would start to cry. The audience will then guess the emotion being portrayed, similar to a game of charades.
Step 2: Create the skit.
Step 3: Practice the skit.
Step 4: Tell the audience who the actors are, where the scene takes place, and what the skit is about. Perform the skit for the class.

Generalization

Instructor reads: It's time for interviews! First pick a partner and practice your interview script one time. I will then inform you who you will be interviewing—options include school personnel, teachers, and other students. Either I will have set up an appointment to interview someone in the building or someone will join us today to be interviewed in the room. Next, complete the interview and ask the person you talked with to rate your interviewing skills on your rating sheets. Last, hand in your rating sheets, and we will have a quick conference about how things went.

The Interview

Student: [Walking up to the person] Excuse me. Do you have a few minutes to help me with a social skills assignment on **the importance of nonverbal communication**?
Student: [If the person says **"no"**] Thank you anyway.
Student: [If the person says **"yes"**] It won't take long, and at the end I will ask you to rate me on a scale of one to five according to how well I do. I won't write anything down, by the way, so I can concentrate on what you are saying. **Let's begin.**

Student: How important is body language in everyday communication? Please explain.
Student: How can you tell how someone may be feeling just by **looking** at the person?
Student: How do **you** communicate with others using body language?
Student: **Thank you.** Now please write your name on the line and rate me on a scale of one to five (one equals poor and five equals excellent), adding comments if you'd like.

Interview Rating

Student's Name ____

Person's Name: ____

Date: ______________________

1. Was I polite when I approached you? ______ (1–5)
2. Did I show that I was listening with my body (using eye contact and standing up straight?) ______ (1–5)
3. Did I use a nice speaking voice? ______ (1–5)
4. Did I make a favorable impression in general? ______ (1–5)

Total score is ______ out of a possible 20.

COMMENTS: ____

Bingo

Instructor reads: It's time for bingo. First I will read off a number and then call on one of you to give an answer, make a comment, or demonstrate a skill. Everyone can cross off the numbers on the bingo sheets as they are called, and you win by getting five in a row. Good luck to you all!

1. Show us angry.
2. Show us happy.
3. Show us annoyed
4. Show us frustrated.
5. Show us content.
6. Show us tired.
7. Show us disappointed.
8. Show us overwhelmed.
9. Show us scared.
10. Show us proud.
11. Show us sad.
12. Show us irate.
13. Show us confused.
14. Show us nervous.
15. Show us surprised.
16. *Time for a skit without words!* Pick a partner and perform a short skit. **Plot:** One person stands too close to the other, who feels uncomfortable and slowly moves away.
17. *Time for a skit without words!* Pick a partner and perform a short skit. **Plot:** One person pretends to cough all over the place and the other person looks grossed out.
18. *Time for a skit without words!* Pick a partner and perform a short skit. **Plot:** One person scares the other person and makes him or her feel surprised and then mad!
19. *Time for a skit without words!* Pick a partner and perform a short skit. **Plot:** One person is crying and the other person comforts him or her until the person stops crying.

20. *Time for a skit without words!* Pick a partner and perform a short skit. **Plot:** One person is afraid of heights; the other tries to convince him or her to climb a ladder and is successful.
21. *Time for a skit without words!* Pick a partner and perform a short skit. **Plot:** A kid drops his mom's expensive bowl and breaks it; his mom gets angry but then cools down.
22. *Time for a skit without words!* Pick a partner and perform a short skit. **Plot:** A kid finishes a running race, and his coach looks happy.
23. *Time for a skit without words!* Pick a partner and perform a short skit. **Plot:** A kid is watching a scary movie and gets very scared, so his mom turns off the TV.
24. *Problem solving:* Jeremy has a problem. No one in his class wants to talk to him because he usually has an angry look on his face and sits up stiff like a statue, making himself appear very unapproachable. List three ways Jeremy can solve his problem, including one negative and two positive solutions.

SKILLS REVIEW

Instructor reads on Monday: Topics to review this week include:

1. Recovery from a Social Mistake
2. Interests: Sharing with Others
3. The Importance of "Plan B"
4. Communication with Body Language

Monday

The plan for the instructor: Host a "show and share" time. Students bring in artifacts or photographs to share with group members, who are seated on chairs in a circle. Each student has up to five minutes to talk about his or her interest while classmates ask questions. Play a board game if there is additional time.

Tuesday

The plan for the instructor: Instruct students to make posters of the review topics. Take photographs of students completing steps of the skills. Make sure each poster includes photographs, key words, and a written guide to the steps used to complete the skill. Display posters in the classroom or around school.

Wednesday

The plan for the instructor: Instruct students to finish their posters and share them with the class. Play a board game if there is additional time.

Thursday

The plan for the instructor: Show classroom videos from the skits. Also show a short video from the Internet—YouTube is often a good source—on one of the review topics: Recovery from a Social Mistake, Interests: Sharing with Others, The Importance of Having a "Plan B," and Communication with Body Language. The students are to watch the video and discuss what they liked about it and tips they learned.

Friday

The plan for the instructor: Play review bingo.

Bingo

Instructor reads: It's time for bingo. First I will read off a number and call on one of you to give an answer, make a comment, or demonstrate a skill. Everyone can cross off the numbers on the bingo sheets as they are called, and you win by getting five in a row.

1. Tell the key points to keep in mind when recovering from a social mistake.
2. Tell the key points to keep in mind when thinking of the importance of "Plan B."
3. Tell the key points to keep in mind when thinking of sharing your interests with others.
4. Tell the key points to remember when communicating using body language.
5. What mistakes should you *avoid* when recovering from a social mistake?
6. What mistakes should you avoid when sharing your interests with others?
7. Under what circumstances might you decide to use a "Plan B"?
8. Why is it a good idea to either walk away quietly or try to change the subject when making a recovery from a social mistake?
9. What can you tell yourself if you make a social mistake and embarrass yourself in public?
10. Give an example of a "Plan B." For example, your plans to go to the movies tonight fell through. What else might you do instead?

11. Give us an example of a "Plan B." For example, you wanted to take a certain class next semester but were unable to because the class was full. What might you do instead?
12. *Share your story:* Tell of a time when you or someone you know made a recovery from a social mistake.
13. *Share your story:* Tell of a time when you focused on talking about someone else's interests instead of your own.
14. *Share your story:* Tell of a time when you communicated with body language.
15. *Share your story:* Tell of a time when you used a "Plan B" when things didn't go your way.
16. How do you feel when you are *unable* to think of a "Plan B"?
17. Why are nonverbal communication skills important?
18. *Time for a nonverbal skit!* **Plot:** With one other person, create a short nonverbal skit on accepting a gift that you really don't like from a friend: First show us the wrong way to do it, then the correct way.
19. *Time for a nonverbal skit!* **Plot:** With another person, create a short nonverbal skit on reacting to a teacher who gives you a bad grade on an assignment: First do it the wrong way, then the correct way.
20. *Time for a skit!* **Plot:** With another person, create a short skit on making up for a social mistake in which you said someone looked like he or she was gaining weight: First do it the wrong way, then the correct way.
21. *Time for a skit!* **Plot:** With another person, create a short skit on sharing your interests with others in a conversation: First do it the wrong way, then the correct way.
22. *Problem solving:* A.J. has a problem. He has a hard time reading other people's nonverbal cues. Just now he is unable to read an expression on his friend's face and is puzzled. List three ways A.J. could solve his problem, including one negative solution and two positive solutions.
23. *Problem solving:* Alicia has a problem. She tries to talk to everyone she knows about video games even when they aren't interested. People are getting bored, and she's losing friends. List three ways Alicia can solve her problem, including one negative and two positive solutions.
24. *Problem solving:* C.J. has a problem. He gets very, very upset if his plans suddenly change or his schedule changes without a lot of notice. List three ways C.J. could deal with his problem, including one negative and two positive solutions.

UNIT THIRTEEN

COMPLIMENTS

Instructor reads: Today's topic has to do with giving and receiving compliments.

Can you think of a time when you either gave a good compliment or received a compliment politely? (Pause) Would anyone be willing to share what happened? (Students respond; instructors can share as well.)

When thinking about compliments, it's good to keep in mind a few characters who can serve as either positive or negative role models.

Character #1 is "Jet the Jerk." Jet generally does not give out compliments unless he feels a person really deserves one. When receiving a compliment he often comes across as being arrogant. For example, if someone comments that he is a good football player, instead of saying "Thank you," he says, "I know I am. That's obvious!"

What do you think of Jet's behavior? (Students respond.)

Character #2 is "Timid Timothy." Timothy comes across as being unaware of both giving and receiving a compliment. When someone gives him a compliment, he most likely argues with the person without realizing that person was trying to say something nice and that he should just say "Thank you." Also, the compliments he gives to others often come out as insults. For example, he may say to an aging man, "Your hair looks pretty good, considering you're going bald."

What do you think of Timothy's behavior? (Students respond.)

Character #3 is "Mature Matt." Mature Matt has gotten pretty good at giving and receiving compliments. If someone gives him a compliment, he has learned to say "Thank you" whether or not he feels like he deserves it or it is true. He does this out of respect for the person who gave the compliment. He also knows how to politely give a compliment. For example, when he notices that his mom has a new haircut, he may say something like, "I like your hair." This is well-received in general because it makes the other person feel good.

What do you think of Matt's behavior? (Students respond.)

In this unit we'll be talking a lot about both receiving and giving compliments. Through practice and self-control, anyone can become like "Mature Matt." The key is to keep working hard on the skill and never give up on yourself. Best wishes to you all!

True or False Quiz

Instructor reads:

1. When someone gives you a compliment about something you're good at, it's polite to say, "I *know* I am!"
2. When someone gives you a sincere compliment, it's polite to say, *"Thank you."*
3. Giving someone a compliment is generally a *nice thing* to do.
4. Sometimes when people give you compliments, it *indicates* that they like you or are interested in you.
5. Compliments are *always* sincere.
6. *Sometimes getting a compliment can make us feel shy or embarrassed.*
7. It's OK to *ignore* someone who gives you a compliment that you feel you don't deserve.
8. It's OK to *argue* with someone about the compliment they give you.

Thumbs-Up or Thumbs-Down

Instructor reads:

1. Someone gives you a compliment by saying, "You are really good at basketball." In reply you say, "No, I'm not. Why would you say such a *stupid* thing?"

2. A star player on your football team receives a compliment and politely says, "Thank you."
3. You *want something* from an acquaintance, so you give that person a compliment.
4. An NFL player receives a compliment and says, "I know. *I'm great!*"
5. You know that a friend of yours is shy about receiving compliments, so you compliment him quietly, not in front of a lot of people.
6. Someone says, "You look nice today." You smile and say, "Thank you. *I'm gorgeous* and I know it!"
7. Someone says, "You look nice today." You say, "Well I should. This is a new shirt, new pants, new belt, new shoes, and a new haircut. I was waiting for someone to notice me!"
8. A kid says to his classmate, "Nice shirt. Where'd you get it, the thrift store?"

Skits

Instructor reads: Practice the following skits with a classmate. Select one skit to be videotaped by your teacher for the class. Words in **bold** are meant to be read with expression. Brackets are used to give acting directions. One student in each group should read the introduction, including the plot, setting, and key concepts, for each skit before choosing actors to portray each role. Good luck!

Skit 1: Giving a Sincere Compliment

Students choose one person to read the introduction before choosing characters and practicing the skit.

INTRODUCTION

Plot: A.J. notices that J.J. is a very good video game player, so he compliments him on his abilities.
Setting: At A.J.'s house
Key concept: Sincere compliments are almost always appreciated.

<u>SKIT</u>

A.J.: [Watching J.J. play a video game] Wow! J.J., you're **great** at this game.

J.J.: Thank you. [Pause] I've been playing it for years.

A.J.: Well, all that work has really paid off. **You're awesome, dude!**

J.J.: Thanks again, but it's really not that hard once you get the hang of it. [Pause] Would you like me to give you some tips?

A.J.: Sure, that would be great!

J.J.: No problem. [Pause] Anytime!

END OF SKIT

Students answer in writing: How can you tell that A.J. is giving a sincere compliment?

Skit 2: Giving a Compliment for Help Received

Students choose one person to read the introduction before choosing characters and practicing the skit.

<u>INTRODUCTION</u>

Plot: J.J. is stuck on a science problem and C.J. helps him, so J.J. gives him a compliment.

Setting: In the science classroom

Key concept: Sincere compliments are usually appreciated.

<u>SKIT</u>

J.J: [Walking over to C.J.'s desk] Hey C.J., do you think you could help me with problem number eight? It's really hard!

C.J.: Oh, sure. [Pause] This one is **really easy** to figure out.

J.J.: Well, I wish I thought that, too. [Pause] Our group is totally stuck on it!

C.J.: [Surprised look] **Seriously?**

J.J.: Yeah. You're **so good** at this kind of stuff. You make it look easy, but it's not really.

C.J.: [Smiling] Well, **thanks** for saying that. [Pause] I guess science has always been an interest of mine, so I don't consider it to be difficult at all.

J.J.: Say, do you think you could point me in the right direction on the next few problems when you're done here?

C.J.: Yeah, sure, no problem. [Walking away] I'll be over in a minute as soon as I've finished up my work.

J.J.: Thanks a lot! You're the best.

END OF SKIT

Students answer in writing: Why might C.J. be surprised to get a compliment about how good he is at science?

Skit 3: An Insincere Compliment

Students choose one person to read the introduction before choosing characters and practicing the skit.

INTRODUCTION

Plot: A.J. compliments C.J. in order to get him to do to do his math problems. The actors are A.J. and C.J.

Setting: In the classroom

Key concept: Beware of compliments that are insincere.

SKIT

A.J.: Hi C.J. [Looking at C.J.'s work] What are you working on there?

C.J.: Oh hi. Just some math. [Pause] I'm almost done though.

A.J.: Really? The homework from yesterday? I'm just starting it, and it's **really hard**. [Pause] You're **so good at math**. I wish I could be **just like you**.

C.J.: Well, thanks. [Pause] I guess I just like math.

A.J.: No, you really are good at it. You're like a math genius!

C.J.: Well, I really wouldn't call myself a genius or anything. But I work hard on it. [Pause] Hey, what exactly are you stuck on? Maybe I can help a bit.

A.J.: Well, I need help on numbers three, six, nine, eleven, thirteen, twenty-one, and twenty-seven.

C.J.: I see. [Pause] That sounds like the **whole** assignment. Let's start with number three. [Looking at the paper and helping with the problem] See, you just do this and carry it out. OK?

A.J.: Well, what I'd really like to **see** are the answers **you've got**.

C.J.: Ah, that's OK. [Pause] I think it would help you more to figure it out on your own.

A.J.: [With an angry voice] Some help **you are**!

C.J.: [Leaving] Well, if you didn't **just want the answers**, I could have helped you. Goodbye!

A.J.: Whatever!
END OF SKIT

Students answer in writing: Why do you think A.J. was giving compliments to C.J.?

Skit 4: Giving a Compliment Just to Be Nice

Students choose one person to read the introduction before choosing characters and practicing the skit.

INTRODUCTION
Plot: J.J. is a good skateboarder, and A.J. mentions that to him.
Setting: At the skate park
Key concept: Sometimes people use compliments just to be friendly.

SKIT
J.J.: Hi, A.J.
A.J.: Oh hi, J.J. What's up?
J.J.: Not much. [Pause] What's up with you?
A.J.: Not too much either. How's your vacation going?
J.J.: Not bad. I seem to be here a lot skateboarding. [Rides around a bit on his skateboard and does a jump.]
A.J.: Hey, you're **really good at that**.
J.J.: Thanks! [Pause] Do you **really** think so?
A.J.: **Absolutely! You're fantastic.** I wish I could do half that stuff.
J.J.: Well, skateboarding is my all-time favorite thing to do.
A.J.: Yeah, you can tell. [Smiling] Well, I have to get going now, but I'll see you around school.
J.J.: Yeah, good talking to you. See ya! [Skating away]
END OF SKIT

Students answer in writing: Why do you think A.J. compliments J.J. on his skateboard abilities?

Group Discussion

Instructor reads: Answer the following questions orally with a partner, then read the steps and design a skit to present to the class.

- What are some of the best compliments you can receive?
- Are there any compliments you *don't* like hearing?
- What's the difference between a *sincere* and an *insincere* compliment
- Why do people give compliments?
- Is it easy or difficult for you to *give* compliments?
- Is it easy or difficult for you to *receive* compliments?
- Do people need compliments? Why or why not?

ORIGINAL SKIT

Step 1: Now, pick a partner and choose a scene in which you either give or receive a compliment. Think about different possibilities, including giving or receiving a compliment with an acquaintance or friend, a teacher, another adult, or a family member.

Step 2: Create the skit.

Step 3: Practice the skit.

Step 4: Tell the audience who the actors are, where the scene takes place, and what the skit is about. Perform the skit for the class.

Generalization

Instructor reads: It's time for interviews! First pick a partner and practice your interview script one time. I will then inform you who you will be interviewing—options include school personnel, teachers, and other students. Either I will have set up an appointment to interview someone in the building or someone will join us today to be interviewed in the room. Next, complete the interview and ask the person you talked with to rate your interviewing skills on your rating sheets. Last, hand in your rating sheets, and we will have a quick conference about how things went.

The Interview

Student: [Walking up to the person] Excuse me. Do you have a few minutes to help me with a social skills assignment on **compliments**?

Student: [If the person says **"no"**] Thank you anyway.

Student: [If the person says **"yes"**] It won't take long, and at the end I will ask you to rate me on a scale of one to five according to how well I do. I won't write anything down, by the way, so I can concentrate on what you are saying. **Let's begin.**

Student: What kinds of compliments do you usually **give**?

Student: What kinds of compliments do you really like to **receive**?

Student: How do you feel when someone gives you a sincere compliment?

Student: **Thank you.** Now please write your name on the line and rate me on a scale of one to five (one equals poor and five equals excellent), adding comments if you'd like to.

Interview Rating

Student's Name ____

Person's Name: ____

Date: ______________________

1. Was I polite when I approached you? ______ (1–5)
2. Did I show that I was listening with my body (using eye contact and standing up straight?) _____ (1–5)
3. Did I use a nice speaking voice? _____ (1–5)
4. Did I make a favorable impression in general? _____ (1–5)

Total score is _____ out of a possible 20.

COMMENTS: ____

____

____

____

____

____

____

____

____

____

____

____

____

____

Bingo

Instructor reads: It's time for bingo. First I will read off a number and then call on one of you to give an answer, make a comment, or demonstrate a skill. Everyone can cross off the numbers on the bingo sheets as they are called, and you win by getting five in a row. Good luck to you all!

1. What kinds of compliments do you usually give?
2. What kinds of compliments do you like to receive?
3. How does it make you feel when you get a sincere compliment?
4. How can you tell if someone is *not* interested in what you are talking about?
5. Demonstrate giving someone in our group a compliment on something he or she is good at.
6. Demonstrate giving someone in our group a compliment about his or her personality.
7. Give an example of an *insincere* compliment.
8. What words could you use to compliment someone's academic ability?
9. What words could you use to compliment someone's basketball skills?
10. What *shouldn't* you do when giving a compliment?
11. What *should* you do when receiving a compliment?
12. *Share your story:* Tell of a time when you received a really nice compliment.
13. Is it easy or difficult for you to give compliments to other people? Explain.
14. What makes for a really great compliment?
15. What was your favorite skit in this unit and why?
16. What compliment might you give your mom or dad?
17. What compliment might you give your friend?
18. What compliment might you give your teacher?
19. What compliment might you give a child?

20. *Why* do people give compliments?
21. What's the absolute *best compliment* you could receive?
22. *Time for a skit!* Pick a partner and perform a short skit. **Plot:** An acquaintance comes up to you and says in a rude tone of voice, "Nice shoes. Where did you them? Walmart?" You respond by saying, "Whatever" and walk away without getting angry. The actors are you and your acquaintance.
23. *Time for a skit!* Pick a partner and perform a short skit. **Plot:** A friend is feeling sad. You give him or her two sincere compliments. The actors are you and your friend.
24. *Problem solving:* Andrea has a problem. Whenever she gets a compliment she says, "No, no, no! That's not true!" She often ends up offending the person who gave her the compliment, and nobody ends up feeling good about it. List three ways Andrea can solve her problem, including one negative and two positive solutions.

UNIT FOURTEEN

PERSONAL RESPONSIBILITY

Instructor reads: Today's topic has to do with taking personal responsibility.

Can you think of a time when you took responsibility for something you said or did? (Pause) Would anyone be willing to share what happened? (Students respond; instructors can share as well.)

When thinking about taking personal responsibility, it's good to keep in mind a few characters who can serve as either positive or negative role models.

Character #1 is "Jet the Jerk." Jet never takes personal responsibility for anything. If he does something wrong, he refuses to admit it and most often blames the mistake on others. For example, say Jet got an F on a test in science because he didn't study. He would most likely say it was the teacher's fault for "not preparing him enough" or making the test "too hard" instead of just admitting that he didn't try.

What do you think of Jet's behavior? (Students respond.)

Character #2 is "Timid Timothy." Timothy takes the opposite approach in that he blames everything on himself in order to gain attention. He takes responsibility loudly for things that are even out of his control. For example, if it rains on the day of the school picnic, he may say something like, "This is all my fault! I wished for rain two days ago, and it finally happened. I'm sorry everyone. I'm sorry!"

What do you think of Timothy's behavior? (Students respond.)

Character #3 is "Mature Matt." Mature Matt is pretty good at accepting personal responsibility. He knows when to say he made an error and when the situation was really out of his control and there was nothing he could have done about it. For example, if Matt is at school and he accidentally tips the teacher's plant over and dirt goes all over the floor, he tells her what happened, apologizes, and then cleans up the mess.

What do you think of Matt's behavior? (Students respond.)

In this unit we'll be talking a lot about taking personal responsibility. Through practice and self-control, anyone can become like "Mature Matt." The key is to keep working hard on the skill and never give up on yourself. Best wishes to you all!

True or False Quiz

Instructor reads:

1. An *example* of taking personal responsibility is apologizing for a mistake you've made.
2. People who take personal responsibility for their actions usually don't whine a lot.
3. It's always easy to take personal responsibility.
4. A person who takes personal responsibility blames everyone *else* for his or her problems.
5. Taking personal responsibility means accepting that while you can't control everything, you can control your own actions and emotions.
6. Sometimes a person doesn't learn to take responsibility for his or her actions because someone like a mom or dad or a friend always comes to the "rescue."
7. People who take personal responsibility tend to feel better about themselves in general than those who don't.
8. Shutting down or sulking—instead of talking about or dealing with a problem—is a form of avoiding personal responsibility.

Thumbs-Up or Thumbs-Down

Instructor reads:

1. You hurt someone's feelings and then refuse to apologize for it.
2. You got an F on a test and blame the teacher for it, even though you didn't study.
3. You lost your library book, so you go to the library and *pay* for it.

4. You have a personal problem. You sit in the hallway at school and cry instead of finding a friend or counselor to talk to.
5. Your friend is upset with you, so you ask him or her what's wrong and how you can help.
6. You find a role model who helps you to figure out ways to take personal responsibility.
7. You're upset with your bad grades, so you blame everyone else for your problems.
8. You decide to take responsibility for your own feelings and actions in everything you do.

Skits

Instructor reads: Practice the following skits with a classmate. Select one skit to be videotaped by your teacher for the class. Words in **bold** are meant to be read with expression. Brackets are used to give acting directions. One student in each group should read the introduction, including the plot, setting, and key concepts, for each skit before choosing actors to portray each role. Good luck!

Skit 1: Refusing to Take Personal Responsibility

Students choose one person to read the introduction before choosing characters and practicing the skit.

INTRODUCTION

Plot: J.J. whines to C.J. about failing grades. The actors are J.J. and C.J. This general plot will also be used in the next skit but with a different outcome.
Setting: In the classroom
Key concept: Whining usually indicates that a person is *not* taking personal responsibility.

SKIT

C.J.: Oh, hi J.J. [Smiling] How are you doing today?

J.J.: [Looking stressed] Not good, not good. [Putting hands on head] **Everything in my life is awful!**
C.J.: What do you mean?
J.J.: [Talking quickly] My mom totally yelled at me this morning because it's midterms and I'm failing all of my classes. [In a whining voice] It's not **my fault** all these teachers grade so hard. I tried to tell my mom, but she wouldn't listen to me, and now I'm grounded for two whole weeks!
C.J.: Aw, that's too bad. [Pause] Do you think you could do something about your grades, like study more or talk to the teachers about extra credit?
J.J.: [Getting louder] What's the use? I'll just fail anyway.
C.J.: So I guess your mind's made up then.
J.J.: Yup.
C.J.: [Frowning] Well, there's nothing I can do for you then if you don't plan to help yourself. [Leaving] See ya.
J.J.: Yeah, see ya. [Fake crying] Boo hoo hoo!
END OF SKIT

Students answer in writing: How does J.J. show that he is unwilling to take responsibility? What does he say?

Skit 2: Taking Personal Responsibility

Students choose one person to read the introduction before choosing characters and practicing the skit.

INTRODUCTION

Plot: J.J. talks to C.J. about why he is failing classes and also about how he can change that. The actors are J.J. and C.J.
Setting: In the classroom
Key concept: It's better to take personal responsibility and come up with a plan for change than to play the role of the victim.

SKIT

C.J: Oh hi, J.J. How are you doing today?
J.J.: [Looking stressed] Not good, not good. [Putting his hands on his head] **Everything in my life is awful!**

C.J.: What do you mean?
J.J.: [Talking quickly] My mom totally yelled at me this morning because it's midterms and I'm failing all my classes. I just don't know what to do about it anymore.
C.J.: **Aw, that's too bad.** [Pause] Do you think you could do something about your grades, like study more or talk to the teachers about extra credit?
J.J.: I could do that. [Pause] But honestly, at times I just don't understand the material.
C.J.: Have you ever thought about coming to study hall for extra help right before or after school? There's a really good teacher in Room 2B who helps kids with **everything**. Sometimes I go there for homework, and it's really not that bad. You get a lot of help, and then you don't have to worry about homework later.
J.J.: [Smiling] Well, I could give it a try. **What have I got to lose, right?**
C.J.: [Smiling] That sounds like a plan! If you'd like, you can stop by my house in the morning, and we can walk down there together.
J.J.: Thanks, I **really** appreciate that.
C.J.: **No problem.** That's what friends are for, right? See ya tomorrow.
J.J.: Yeah, see ya.
END OF SKIT

Students answer in writing: What does J.J. do to take personal responsibility in this case?

Skit 3: Paying for a Mistake

Students choose one person to read the introduction before choosing characters and practicing the skit.

INTRODUCTION

Plot: A.J. has crashed his four-wheeler and is responsible to pay for the damages. He asks his neighbor, Mrs. Josephson, if she has any jobs around the house that he could do to earn money. The actors are A.J. and Mrs. Josephson.
Setting: At Mrs. Josephson's front door
Key concept: Taking responsibility sometimes means paying your own money for a mistake.

SKIT

A.J.: [A.J. knocks on the door; Mrs. Josephson answers it] Hi, Mrs. Josephson.

Mrs. Josephson: Oh hi, A.J. [Pause] What brings you here?
A.J.: Well, to tell you the truth, I crashed my four-wheeler, and now I have to **pay** to get it fixed. I don't have a lot of money, so I'm trying to find some odd jobs to do to help pay it off.
Mrs. Josephson: **Oh really?**
A.J.: Yeah. So I was wondering if maybe you have a lawnmowing job, painting, or some other types of jobs I could do to earn a little money.
Mrs. Josephson: Hmmm. [Pause] Let me think. Well, there is that tree in the yard that fell down in the storm a couple of weeks ago. My husband plans to cut it up and haul it away this weekend. I'll ask him if he needs some help with that and give you a call.
A.J.: Thanks a lot. I **really** appreciate it.
Mrs. Josephson: No problem. By the way, how much is it going to cost to fix the four-wheeler?
A.J.: About six hundred dollars.
Mrs. Josephson: [Looking shocked] **Whew, that's a lot of money.** Good thing you're ambitious.
A.J.: [Smiling] I've gotta be going. Thanks again. See ya, Mrs. Josephson.
Mrs. Josephson: Yeah, we'll see you again soon!
END OF SKIT

Students answer in writing: What does A.J. do to take personal responsibility?

Skit 4: Someone Tries to Pass His Responsibility on to You

Students choose one person to read the introduction before choosing characters and practicing the skit.

INTRODUCTION

Plot: C.J. asks A.J. for lunch money **again**, but A.J. doesn't give it to him because that's not his responsibility.
Setting: In the cafeteria at school
Key concept: Beware that some people may try to get you to do things for them that are actually their own responsibility—not yours!

SKIT

C.J.: [Smiling] Hi there, A.J.

A.J.: Oh, hi. What's up? [Looking annoyed] I suppose you're going to ask me for lunch money again, huh?
C.J.: Just for today. [Pleading] **Please?** I promise to pay you back.
A.J.: That's what you've been saying the last **three days in a row**. When you pay me back what you already owe me we can talk about future loans. [Speaking angrily] **Until that time, the bank of A.J. is officially closed!**
C.J.: Why do you have to be such a *jerk*?
A.J.: I am **not** being a jerk actually. [Pause] You're not being responsible, and that's **your** problem, **not mine**.
C.J.: [Leaving] **Whatever.**
A.J.: OK, whatever then.
END OF SKIT

Students answer in writing: Why did this conversation didn't go so well?

Group Discussion

Instructor reads: Answer the following questions orally with a partner, then read the steps and design a skit to present to the class.

- What are your responsibilities at home?
- What are your responsibilities at school?
- What are your responsibilities if you feel hurt or upset?
- What can you do to *show* that you are taking responsibility for your behavior or actions?
- What is the *opposite* of taking personal responsibility? Explain.
- Are you responsible for your thoughts and actions? Why or why not?
- Are you responsible for *other people's* thoughts and actions? Why or why not?

ORIGINAL SKIT

Step 1: With a partner, choose a scene in which you take personal responsibility for something you have said or done that was wrong. Think about different possibilities, including taking responsibility for your actions with an acquaintance or friend, a teacher or another adult, or a family member.

Step 2: Create the skit.
Step 3: Practice the skit.
Step 4: Tell the audience who the actors are, where the scene takes place, and what the skit is about. Perform the skit for the class.

Generalization

Instructor reads: It's time for interviews! First pick a partner and practice your interview script one time. I will then inform you who you will be interviewing—options include school personnel, teachers, and other students. Either I will have set up an appointment to interview someone in the building or someone will join us today to be interviewed in the room. Next, complete the interview and ask the person you talked with to rate your interviewing skills on your rating sheets. Last, hand in your rating sheets, and we will have a quick conference about how things went.

The Interview

Student: [Walking up to the person] Excuse me. Do you have a few minutes to help me with a social skills assignment on **taking personal responsibility**?
Student: [If the person says **"no"**] Thank you anyway.
Student: [If the person says **"yes"**] It won't take long, and at the end I will ask you to rate me on a scale of one to five according to how well I do. I won't write anything down, by the way, so I can concentrate on what you are saying. **Let's begin.**
Student: What does **taking personal responsibility** mean to you?
Student: Why should a person take personal responsibility for his or her words and actions?
Student: What happens when someone at work or at home **doesn't** take personal responsibility?
Student: **Thank you.** Now please write your name on the line and rate me on a scale of one to five (one equals poor and five equals excellent), adding comments if you'd like.

Interview Rating

Student's Name ______________________________

Person's Name: ______________________________

Date: ____________________

1. Was I polite when I approached you? _______ (1–5)
2. Did I show that I was listening with my body (using eye contact and standing up straight?) ______ (1–5)
3. Did I use a nice speaking voice? ______ (1–5)
4. Did I make a favorable impression in general? ______ (1–5)

Total score is ______ out of a possible 20.

COMMENTS: ______________________________

Bingo

Instructor reads: It's time for bingo. First I will read off a number and then call on one of you to give an answer, make a comment, or demonstrate a skill. Everyone can cross off the numbers on the bingo sheets as they are called, and you win by getting five in a row. Good luck to you all!

1. What does taking personal responsibility mean to you?
2. Give an example of someone taking personal responsibility.
3. Are you responsible for yourself and your actions? Explain.
4. Give an example of the *opposite* of taking personal responsibility.
5. Tell how you can show responsibility with a pet.
6. Tell how you can take responsibility for your belongings.
7. Tell how you demonstrate personal responsibility to yourself.
8. Give an example of how a person might try to get *others* to take responsibility for what he or she actually did.
9. How can you take personal responsibility in school?
10. How can you take personal responsibility at home?
11. How can you take personal responsibility in the community?
12. What was your favorite skit in this unit and why?
13. Show with your body how you would communicate taking responsibility for an action. How would you stand or sit?
14. How can you show personal responsibility at a job?
15. If you have a personal problem that keeps you from performing well at school, what could you do?
16. When someone demands your time, money, or attention, what can you do?
17. When you have a problem and you have the ability to solve it, what should you do?
18. What are some of our responsibilities as citizens of the United States?
19. What sorts of things are other people's responsibilities, not yours?
20. Are you good at taking personal responsibility? Explain.

21. What words could you use to take responsibility for breaking your grandmother's vase?
22. What words could you use to take responsibility for not doing your homework on time?
23. *Time for a skit!* Pick a partner and perform a short skit. **Plot:** A student is asking you to do the homework for him or her. You know that this is not your responsibility, and you respond appropriately. The actors are you and the other student.
24. *Problem solving:* Kari has a problem. Her mom catches her telling a lie about cleaning her room, but she still denies it. List three ways Kari can solve her problem, including one negative and two positive solutions.

COMMUNITY PRACTICE

Instructor Preparation for the Tour

1. Choose a place to visit in the community and arrange for a tour. Explain who your group is, what they will do there, and what they hope to learn. Options include a store, a bank, a hotel, a police station, a hospital, or a local newspaper.
2. Discuss with the class what they can expect to see on the tour and review behavioral expectations.
3. If possible, watch a short video to preview a place similar to the one you will be visiting. (YouTube is a good resource for short videos.)
4. Instruct the students to practice self-introductions.
5. Instruct the students to think of and practice two questions they might ask of the guide while on the tour (one question after the introduction and one question sometime throughout the tour).
6. Designate a student leader to give the greeting upon arrival as well as the closing remarks.

Student Expectations During the Tour

1. When arriving, the student leader says to the guide, "Hi! We're here for the tour."
2. All students then make an introduction, starting with the student leader.

3. All students ask two questions of the guide, one after the introductions and one sometime throughout the tour.
4. At the end, the student leader says, "Thank you for the tour."
5. All students write thank you notes and send them to the guide.

Option for Self-Introduction Practice Without Taking a Tour

Invite community leaders whom students either don't know or don't know well to come to your room for one class. Examples of potential guests include police officers, firefighters, journalists, business leaders, or others. Explain to the guests how the class will be structured. Students should be seated around the room next to an empty chair. Guests will be welcomed in and will be asked to sit next to a student. Set a timer for two minutes, allowing for both the student and the guest to give an introduction and share a bit about themselves. Students should be cued to ask two questions of the guest, such as "What does a typical day at your job look like?" or "What do you like about your job?" When the timer goes off, guests will be asked to move clockwise around the room. When the students have met all the guests, the students will thank the guests for coming and sit back down in their chairs. Review how the interviews went and what students learned from the guests. Students then also write follow-up thank you cards to be sent to the guests.

UNIT FIFTEEN

SHARING TOO MUCH INFORMATION

Instructor reads: Today's topic has to do with sharing too much information, sometimes called "TMI."

Can you think of a time when you or someone you know shared too much information too soon after meeting? (Pause) Would anyone be willing to share what happened? (Students respond; instructors can share as well.)

When thinking about sharing too much information, it's good to keep in mind a few characters who can serve as either positive or negative role models.

Character #1 is "Jet the Jerk." Jet doesn't care what he shares with others, even if it is personal and makes other people feel uncomfortable. For example, if he returns to school after a doctor's appointment for a stomach problem, he tells the entire class—including the teacher—all about his bathroom experiences as well as what happened in the doctor's office.

What do you think of Jet's behavior? (Students respond.)

Character #2 is "Timid Timothy." Timothy tells too much information right away because he doesn't understand that personal information is shared generally only *after* getting to know someone, and in the right setting. For example, if a new student comes to class, Timothy shares information right away about where he lives, what he likes to do, and details about his family life as well as his private health records. He often doesn't understand that this type of oversharing makes others shy away from him.

What do you think of Timothy's behavior? (Students respond.)

Character #3 is "Mature Matt." Mature Matt knows how much information to share with others. He knows that while talking to his best friend about personal issues in private is perfectly acceptable, he would never share that same information with a room full of strangers.

What do you think of Matt's behavior? (Students respond.)

In this unit we'll be talking a lot about when and where to share information. Through practice and self-control, anyone can become like "Mature Matt." The key is to keep working hard on the skill and never give up on yourself. Best wishes to you all!

True or False Quiz

Instructor reads:

1. An *example* of too much information is when you meet someone you think is cute, and you *go on and on* about your personal information.
2. An example of too much information is when you talk to someone you've just met about the kinds of music you like.
3. It's never a good idea to share personal information on the Internet.
4. Sharing too much information with another person after you've just met them can make that person feel uncomfortable.
5. Telling someone what color underwear you are wearing may be too much information.
6. Telling someone in detail about the last time you were sick may be too much information.
7. Telling someone your phone number may be too much information.
8. It's considered OK to tell a person where you are from when meeting them for the first time.

Thumbs-Up or Thumbs-Down

Instructor reads:

1. You *just met* someone and you tell the person all about your family issues and problems.
2. You talk in private to a counselor about a personal problem that's bothering you.
3. You announce to the whole class that your parents are getting a divorce.
4. You get injured by a ball in your private parts and you *yell* that information out for the world to hear.
5. You tell your good friend about why you've been so sad lately.
6. You sit by someone you don't know at lunch and tell the person *every detail* about yourself.
7. An adult at school—who is *not* the nurse—asks you personal questions about your health and you tell all.
8. A friend of a friend asks you why you stopped dating a certain person, and you tell him that it's *none* of his business.

Skits

Instructor reads: Practice the following skits with a classmate. Select one skit to be videotaped by your teacher for the class. Words in **bold** are meant to be read with expression. Brackets are used to give acting directions. One student in each group should read the introduction, including the plot, setting, and key concepts, for each skit before choosing actors to portray each role. Good luck!

Skit 1: Sharing Too Much Information in the Cafeteria (What Not to Do)

Students choose one person to read the introduction before choosing characters and practicing the skit.

INTRODUCTION

Plot: C.J. has a personal problem with acne and he announces this loudly in the lunchroom. The actors are C.J. and A.J.

Setting: In the cafeteria at a table

Key concept: Information about body or health issues should be kept private.

SKIT

C.J.: [Smiling] How's your day going?

A.J.: [Smiling] Oh pretty good. And you?

C.J.: [Talking very loudly] It's good, but I am really, really bothered by this big huge zit on my nose. I wish I could pop it right now and have it explode all over!

A.J.: [Looking shocked] That's just **gross**, C.J.! [Speaking quietly] Ah, you may want to talk a little quieter. [Pause] People are starting to stare.

C.J.: Who cares? [Standing up and yelling] I hate my huge zit! I hate my stupid life! I'm going to pop this zit right now!

A.J.: [Motioning for C.J. to sit down] **Hey, hey now. Let's just sit down and calm down a bit.** Other people are staring. How about after lunch we go and talk somewhere in private?

C.J.: [Sitting down] Yeah, I guess you're right. I **am** sort of being obnoxious. It's just that I'm so **stressed out** lately, and this zit is really pushing me over the edge.

A.J.: I can understand that. How about if we finish up these burgers and go outside and talk in private? That might help.

C.J.: [Smiling] It couldn't be any worse than making a fool of myself in front of everyone.

A.J.: [Smiling] You know you're right about **that**!

C.J.: I **am** right, and it feels **good**! [Pause] Now let's finish these burgers and get out of here.

A.J.: [Getting up to leave] Sounds good to me!

END OF SKIT

Students answer in writing: What did C.J. do in this skit that caused his friend to feel embarrassed?

Skit 2: Sharing Information in Private with a Friend

Students choose one person to read the introduction before choosing characters and practicing the skit.

INTRODUCTION

Plot: J.J. has a personal problem with acne. He waits until he can talk about it with C.J. in private. The actors are J.J. and C.J.

Setting: In the hallway at classroom

Key concept: Discuss private issues in private with someone you trust.

SKIT

J.J.: [Walking down the hall and meeting C.J.] Oh, hi C.J. [Smiling] How's it going? I've been looking **all over** for you.

C.J.: [Smiling] Oh really? What's up?

J.J.: [Talking quietly] Well, I'd really like to talk to you in private. Do you have a minute? [Walking to the end of the hallway where there is no one around] Look at me **closely**. Do you notice anything strange about me?

C.J.: [Looking at J.J.'s face] Not really; just a little bump that looks like a zit or something. Am I supposed to see something more?

J.J.: [Smiling] So my huge zit isn't that noticeable? [Pause] I tried to cover it up with my mom's makeup this morning—maybe that helped.

C.J.: No, I really don't see much of anything. It must blend in pretty well—I can barely even see it.

J.J.: **Well, that's a relief!** I worried about that stupid thing all day and could have sworn it was big, red, ugly, and just about the size of **Canada**.

C.J.: So it's no big deal then, right? But I know what you mean about being worried about zits. They're so **gross**!

J.J.: I agree. [Pause] Well, thanks for the help. Call me later and maybe we can do something.

C.J.: [Leaving] Sounds good. See ya.

J.J.: Yeah, see ya!

END OF SKIT

Students answer in writing: Why was it a good idea for J.J. to ask to talk to C.J. in private?

Skit 3: Sharing Too Much Too Soon (What Not to Do)

Students choose one person to read the introduction before choosing characters and practicing the skit.

INTRODUCTION

Plot: C.J. recently just met A.J. but decides to share personal information with him anyway. The actors are C.J. and A.J.

Setting: At school during breakfast

Key concept: Sharing a lot of personal information too soon can make others feel uncomfortable.

SKIT

C.J.: [Smiling and walking up to J.J. at the breakfast table] Oh hi, A.J. How's it going? **Do you want to hang out?**

A.J.: [Smiling] I suppose I have a bit of time before class, sure. You can sit here if you'd like.

C.J.: [Sitting down] Well, I really liked meeting you last week, and I was going to call you about five times on Saturday, but I was afraid you wouldn't want to talk to me.

A.J.: [Looking surprised] Why's that?

C.J.: Well, sometimes people say I come on **too strong** by giving out a bunch of personal information too fast.

A.J.: Oh really?

C.J.: [Talking quickly] Yeah, by the way, did I mention that my parents are divorced, I have two sisters who I fight with all the time, and that I was held back from kindergarten twice?

A.J.: [Looking uncomfortable] **No**, you didn't mention that.

C.J.: [Talking even more quickly] Yeah, and I love the color yellow but hate egg noodles. Well, I only really hate them if they don't have enough butter and salt. If they have lots of butter and salt then I **love** them. I also love spaghetti and lasagna—basically anything with noodles.

A.J.: [Leaving] Hey, not to be rude or anything, but I have to get going.

C.J.: See you some other time then?

A.J.: Yeah, **maybe**. [Leaving] Bye now.

C.J.: [Looking sad] Bye. [Pause] Looks like I did it again!

END OF SKIT

Students answer in writing: What was C.J.'s mistake in this skit?

Skit 4: Sharing Too Much with the Wrong Person (What Not to Do)

Students choose one person to read the introduction before choosing characters and practicing the skit.

INTRODUCTION

Plot: A.J. shares too much information with the school gossip, J.J. The actors are A.J. and J.J.
Setting: At school
Key concept: Be careful not to share personal information with someone who gossips a lot.

SKIT

A.J.: [Walking over to J.J. in the hallway] Oh hi, J.J. What are you up to?
J.J.: Not much. Just chilling out. [Smiling sweetly] What's **new** with you?
A.J.: Oh, there's **a lot** going on with me right now. Two nights ago I got so mad that I punched a hole in my bedroom door and broke my arm—see. People are wondering if I need some psychological help.
J.J.: [Looking very interested] Oh, really? That sounds **scary**. Do you usually blow up like that?
A.J.: Sometimes [Pause] Not every time I get mad though.
J.J.: [Leaving] Well, I have to run now and make some phone calls to a few people who **also like to know** what's going on around this school. Good luck with your arm.
A.J.: Thanks [Pause] It still really hurts. See you around!
J.J.: Yeah, bye.
END OF SKIT

Students answer in writing: Why didn't this conversation go well?

Group Discussion

Instructor reads: Answer the following questions orally with a partner, then read the steps and design a skit to present to the class.

- What topics are generally considered *too much information* to share with anyone other than family or close friends?
- When do you hear too much information from others?
- What kinds of topics are generally acceptable to talk about with anyone?
- How might someone feel if you share too much information right away?
- How can you tell if it's OK to share personal information with somebody?
- What can you say to someone who shares too much information with you?
- How has the Internet influenced how we share information?

ORIGINAL SKIT

Step 1: With a partner, choose a scene in which you share too much information and the other person gets uncomfortable and walks away. Think about different possibilities, including sharing too much at school, in a public setting such as an auditorium, or with someone you just met.
Step 2: Create the skit.
Step 3: Practice the skit.
Step 4: Tell the audience who the actors are, where the scene takes place, and what the skit is about. Perform the skit for the class.

Generalization

Instructor reads: It's time for interviews! First pick a partner and practice your interview script one time. I will then inform you who you will be interviewing—options include school personnel, teachers, and other students. Either I will have set up an appointment to interview someone in the building or someone will join us today to be interviewed in the room. Next, complete the interview and ask the person you talked with to rate your interviewing skills on your rating sheets. Last, hand in your rating sheets, and we will have a quick conference about how things went.

The Interview

Student: [Walking up to the person] Excuse me. Do you have a few minutes to help me with a social skills assignment on **the concept of "too much information," or TMI**?
Student: [If the person says **"no"**] Thank you anyway.
Student: [If the person says **"yes"**] It won't take long, and at the end I will ask you to rate me on a scale of one to five according to how well I do. I won't write anything down, by the way, so I can concentrate on what you are saying. **Let's begin.**
Student: What do you consider to be "too much information" to hear about a person when you've just met him or her?
Student: Has anyone ever told you too much information too soon upon meeting for the first time? If so, how did that make you feel?
Student: What kinds of things wouldn't you talk about with someone you didn't know well?
Student: **Thank you.** Now please write your name on the line and rate me on a scale of one to five (one equals poor and five equals excellent), adding comments if you'd like.

Interview Rating

Student's Name ______________________________

Person's Name: ______________________________

Date: ____________________

1. Was I polite when I approached you? ______ (1–5)
2. Did I show that I was listening with my body (using eye contact and standing up straight?) _____ (1–5)
3. Did I use a nice speaking voice? _____ (1–5)
4. Did I make a favorable impression in general? _____ (1–5)

Total score is _____ out of a possible 20.

COMMENTS: ______________________________

Bingo

Instructor reads: It's time for bingo. First I will read off a number and then call on one of you to give an answer, make a comment, or demonstrate a skill. Everyone can cross off the numbers on the bingo sheets as they are called, and you win by getting five in a row. Good luck to you all!

1. What is your definition of sharing too much information?
2. How do you know when you've shared too much information?
3. Give an example of a topic you *wouldn't* share with someone you had just met.
4. Give an example of one topic you might discuss in private with a trusted adult or the school nurse.
5. How might it make a person feel if you share too much information with him or her shortly after you just met?
6. What are two reasons to keep some of your thoughts private?
7. What words could you use to tell someone that you don't want to hear so much private information?
8. What words could you use to tell someone that you don't feel comfortable answering his or her question?
9. Why is it important to use good timing when sharing personal information with someone?
10. Who can you share personal information with?
11. *Where* might you share private information?
12. What might be an appropriate *time* to share private information?
13. Why do people sometimes share too much information?
14. What was your favorite skit in this unit and why?
15. Is giving out your phone number sharing too much information? Explain.
16. Is talking about details of a doctor's appointment sharing too much information? Explain.
17. Show with body language how you would communicate that you are uncomfortable with what that person is talking about.

18. What are some general "safe" topics you can talk about when you don't know someone well?
19. How can you tell when you've just shared too much information? Explain.
20. Demonstrate politely telling someone that he or she is sharing too much information.
21. Demonstrate politely telling someone that the information he or she is asking for is your own private business.
22. *Share your story:* Have you ever talked to someone who shared too much information with you? Explain.
23. *Time for a skit!* Pick a partner and perform a short skit. **Plot:** You are at a party and you meet someone for the first time. You start sharing too much information about the details of your health and end up making the other person feel uncomfortable. The actors are you and the person you talk to.
24. *Problem solving:* Kari has a problem. Whenever she meets someone new, she shares way too much personal information without first getting to know the person. List three ways Kari can solve her problem, including one negative and two positive solutions.

UNIT SIXTEEN

THE ACT OF PRETENDING NOT TO NOTICE

Instructor reads: Today's topic has to do with situations in which it is acceptable to pretend not to notice what is happening so as to not be nosy or cause others embarrassment.

Can you think of a time when you pretended not to notice something? (Pause) Would anyone be willing to share what happened? (Students respond; instructors can share as well.)

When thinking about sharing too much information, it's good to keep in mind a few characters who can serve as either positive or negative role models.

Character #1 is "Jet the Jerk." Jet generally notices and makes comments on most things he sees, no matter how much he might embarrass someone or pry into someone's business. For example, if he is in line at the bank and he hears that the customer in line ahead of him has only ten dollars left in his bank account, he would think nothing of saying rather loudly, "Sounds like you're almost broke!" as the person turns to leave.

What do you think of Jet's behavior? (Students respond.)

Character #2 is "Timid Timothy." At times, Timothy tries to ignore things that happen, but he is no good at it. For example, if a classmate has a really red lump on his nose, Timothy wouldn't come right out and stare at it, but he would keep peeking to see it, making it obvious that he was looking at it.

What do you think of Timothy's behavior? (Students respond.)

Character #3 is "Mature Matt." Matt is good at knowing when he should pretend not to notice something. He knows that sometimes it is good to ignore things and mind your own business. For example, when he sees or hears something such as two classmates getting into an argument, he doesn't join in, stare, or tell other people about what happened, because it doesn't concern him.

What do you think of Matt's behavior? (Students respond.)

In this unit we'll be talking a lot about the act of pretending not to notice. Through practice and self-control, anyone can become like "Mature Matt." The key is to keep working hard on the skill and never give up on yourself. Best wishes to you all!

True or False Quiz

Instructor reads:

1. If a stranger enters the room wearing a cast, it is generally not polite to stare and ask, "What happened to you?"
2. If a friend walks in with a black eye, it's appropriate to ask what happened because you know the person well.
3. It's always important to comment about *everything* you observe in public.
4. When witnessing a situation that makes people feel uncomfortable, it's usually OK to just ignore it.
5. If you notice something about a person—like a particularly bad haircut—it's polite *not* to mention it.
6. What you say to others or how much you get involved in their business often depends on your relationship with that person.
7. It's generally considered rude to comment on others' acne.
8. It's generally considered rude to make comments about a person's body.

Thumbs-Up or Thumbs-Down

Instructor reads:

1. You meet someone whom you haven't seen for a while, and you notice that he has gained weight, so you say, "Wow! You've really *packed on some pounds*!"
2. Your friend's mom comes over for lunch. She's wearing a really ugly outfit, and you immediately tell her how hideous it looks.
3. You notice a stranger with a prosthetic leg, so you ask about it.
4. Your good friend has a piece of broccoli stuck on her teeth, so you gently tell her about it in private.
5. You notice that a classmate's zipper is down, but you are seated far away from him and don't want to cause a scene, so you ignore it.
6. You are working at a movie theater and someone comes in wearing a toupee that appears to be falling off his head. You pretend *not* to notice.
7. You just met someone who has a funny laugh, so you comment about it by saying, "That's some *weird laugh* you have!"
8. Your good friend looks pale and sick, so you ask her if she's OK.

Skits

Instructor reads: Practice the following skits with a classmate. Select one skit to be videotaped by your teacher for the class. Words in **bold** are meant to be read with expression. Brackets are used to give acting directions. One student in each group should read the introduction, including the plot, setting, and key concepts, for each skit before choosing actors to portray each role. Good luck!

Skit 1: Ignoring a Bad Haircut

Students choose one person to read the introduction before choosing characters and practicing the skit.

INTRODUCTION

Plot: J.J. just got a bad haircut, but A.J. chooses not to say anything about it because he doesn't know J.J. well. The actors are J.J. and A.J.

Setting: In the classroom at school

Key concept: Sometimes the most polite thing you can do is to pretend not to notice.

SKIT

A.J.: Oh, hi J.J. [Sitting at the desk] How are you?

J.J.: Not bad. [Smiling] I see we have another huge history assignment.

A.J.: Yeah. This teacher really loves to pile on the homework. [Pause] I guess he doesn't like kids or something.

J.J.: Hey, [Pause] **can I ask you something**? Is it very obvious that I got a **really bad haircut** this weekend? I mean, can you tell half my hair is shaved off on one side?

A.J.: Well, I did notice it, but I thought you just liked your hair **really, really** short in places.

J.J.: To tell you the truth, I don't really like short hair at all. It's just that my dad got a little crazy with the clippers and then ended up having to shave part of it off to try to fix it. Next time, for sure, I'm going to a **real** barber. **I'm so embarrassed.**

A.J.: Aw, don't worry about it! [Smiling] I'll bet in about two weeks you won't even be able to tell.

J.J.: Really?

A.J.: Yeah. That's about how long it took for me to grow my hair out after a really bad haircut a while back.

J.J.: I can't wait until it looks decent again. [Pause] Anyway, thanks for listening. [Smiling]

A.J.: Now onto that history project!

J.J.: Yeah. [Smiling and opening up his book] History is a great way to get my mind off my hair!

END OF SKIT

Students answer in writing: How did A.J. act politely in this skit?

Skit 2: Pretending Not to Notice in the Grocery Store

Students choose one person to read the introduction before choosing characters and practicing the skit.

Introduction

Plot: C.J. is working as a clerk in a grocery store. A man comes through his line with lipstick kisses on his face. C.J. pretends not to notice. The actors are C.J. and the customer.
Setting: In the checkout counter at the grocery store
Key concept: Sometimes the most polite thing you can do is to pretend not to notice.

Skit

C.J.: How are you doing today? [Smiling at the man and looking down] Did you find everything all right?
Man.: Good, thanks. [Smiling] And yes I did.
C.J.: [Checking out the rest of the groceries while looking at the items and not the man] That'll be twenty-nine ninety-five.
Man: [Handing over the money] Here's thirty dollars.
C.J.: And five cents is your change. [Smiling] Thanks and have a nice day.
Man: [Leaving with the groceries] Thanks, you too.
End of skit

Students answer in writing: How did C.J. ignore the lipstick kisses? What did he do?

Skit 3: Bringing Up Something You Should Have Ignored (What Not to Do)

Students choose one person to read the introduction before choosing characters and practicing the skit.

Introduction

Plot: A.J. is sitting at the table when J.J. comes over to sit by him. J.J. has lost a lot of weight recently, and A.J. makes a big deal about it, even though he doesn't know J.J. well. The actors are A.J. and J.J.
Setting: In the cafeteria
Key concept: Sometimes it's best not to point out the obvious if you don't know a person well.

<u>SKIT</u>

J.J.: Oh, hi, A.J. [Smiling] Is anyone going to be sitting here?

A.J.: No, have a seat. [Smiling] It's J.J., right? And what's this I hear about you going on this big diet and losing forty pounds or something like that? **That's awesome! How did you do it? Diet, exercise, shakes, or something?**

J.J.: [Speaking quietly] Actually, to tell you the truth, I have this rare **disease** and it's causing me to lose weight rapidly. No one seems to know what it is or how to control it.

A.J.: Oh, really? [Looking shocked] Hey, look, I'm really sorry that I brought it up. [Pause] I hope that didn't make you feel **weird** or anything.

J.J.: No, it's OK. [Pause] I just don't like talking about it much.

A.J.: I see. [Looking concerned] I won't bring it up again. I'm really sorry.

J.J.: No big deal. [Pause] Now can you pass me the salt?

END OF SKIT

Students answer in writing: What does A.J. mention that he shouldn't have?

Skit 4: When It's OK to Notice Something

Students choose one person to read the introduction before choosing characters and practicing the skit.

<u>INTRODUCTION</u>

Plot: C.J. is in the cafeteria with a good friend named J.J. J.J. will do anything **not** to feel embarrassed in public. C.J. notices something wrong and points it out to him quietly. The actors are C.J. and J.J.

Setting: At a lunch table in the cafeteria

Key concept: If you know a person well, it's OK to notice and say something about things that are potentially embarrassing.

<u>SKIT</u>

C.J.: [Walking over to sit down] Oh hi, J.J. [Pause] How are you today?

J.J.: Great, just great!

C.J.: [Looking at a piece of spinach stuck to his front tooth] Ah, I don't know how to tell you this, but you have a big green piece of spinach stuck right on your tooth here. [Points to J.J.'s tooth]

J.J.: [Looking surprised] Really? [Pause] Show me where it is, quick, so I can get it off.
C.J.: [Pointing to where it is] It's right there.
J.J.: Thanks for telling me. [Picks off teeth] Did I get it? I'd better go to a mirror and check it out.
C.J.: Don't worry about it now, it's gone. [Smiling] You look like a rock star.
J.J.: [Speaking quickly] Thank goodness you **told** me. I have to give a speech in my next class, and if it would have been there, I would have absolutely **died** of embarrassment. [Looking relieved] Thanks so much; you're the best.
C.J.: No big deal. [Pause] That's what friends are for, right?
J.J.: Right. [Leaving] Well, have a good one. I'll see you later.
C.J.: Yeah, see ya.
END OF SKIT

Students answer in writing: Why was it good for C.J. to point out the spinach in this case?

Group Discussion

Instructor reads: Answer the following questions orally with a partner, then read the steps and design a skit to present to the class.

- Name two things you should ignore when you notice them in public.
- What kinds of things *shouldn't* you ignore in public?
- What are some things that are OK to notice and talk about in public?
- Do you think anyone's ever ignored something about you? Explain.
- Do you have to comment on everything you notice? Explain.
- Why do we often choose to ignore things we notice?
- What would it be like if everyone mentioned everything in public?

<u>Original Skit</u>

Step 1: With a partner, choose a scene in which you ignore something unusual in a public place. Think about different possibilities, including something you observe at school, at a restaurant, or in the community. Your partner will do the unusual thing such as hiccup loudly or swat at a bug.

Step 2: Create the skit.

Step 3: Practice the skit.

Step 4: Tell the audience who the actors are, where the scene takes place, and what the skit is about. Perform the skit for the class.

Generalization

Instructor reads: It's time for interviews! First pick a partner and practice your interview script one time. I will then inform you who you will be interviewing—options include school personnel, teachers, and other students. Either I will have set up an appointment to interview someone in the building or someone will join us today to be interviewed in the room. Next, complete the interview and ask the person you talked with to rate your interviewing skills on your rating sheets. Last, hand in your rating sheets, and we will have a quick conference about how things went.

The Interview

Student: [Walking up to the person] Excuse me. Do you have a few minutes to help me with a social skills assignment on **the act of pretending not to notice something in public**?

Student: [If the person says **"no"**] Thank you anyway.

Student: [If the person says **"yes"**] It won't take long, and at the end I will ask you to rate me on a scale of one to five according to how well I do. I won't write anything down, by the way, so I can concentrate on what you are saying. **Let's begin.**

Student: Do you ever purposely ignore something you observe in public? If so, will you please tell me about it?

Student: Do you ever warn your friends of something embarrassing, like if their zipper is down or they have food stuck on their teeth? Please explain why if so.

Student: Why do we sometimes **choose** to ignore some of the things we see in public?
Student: **Thank you.** Now please write your name on the line and rate me on a scale of one to five (one equals poor and five equals excellent), adding comments if you'd like.

Interview Rating

Student's Name ______________________________

Person's Name: ______________________________

Date: ______________

1. Was I polite when I approached you? _______ (1–5)
2. Did I show that I was listening with my body (using eye contact and standing up straight?) ______ (1–5)
3. Did I use a nice speaking voice? ______ (1–5)
4. Did I make a favorable impression in general? ______ (1–5)

Total score is ______ out of a possible 20.

COMMENTS: ______________________________

Bingo

Instructor reads: It's time for bingo. First I will read off a number and then call on one of you to give an answer, make a comment, or demonstrate a skill. Everyone can cross off the numbers on the bingo sheets as they are called, and you win by getting five in a row. Good luck to you all!

1. *Should you* try to ignore certain things you see in public? Explain.
2. What are two things that are easy for you to ignore in public?
3. What are two things that are *difficult* for you to ignore in public?
4. What are some things you might observe that you shouldn't ignore?
5. Demonstrate the opposite of ignoring that someone's zipper is down. Talk about it loudly!
6. Demonstrate with body language how you could ignore someone coughing loudly next to you on a city bus.
7. What polite words could you use if a good friend had broccoli all over his or her teeth?
8. What polite words could you use if a good friend's hair was sticking up all over?
9. What is the polite thing to do if you notice a group of people in wheelchairs at the mall?
10. What is the polite thing to do if you notice a young mother struggling to hold a toddler who is screaming and crying at the grocery store?
11. What is the polite thing to do if you notice that someone you don't know personally has a skin rash all over?
12. What is the polite thing to do if you notice a child with pudding all over his face at the library?
13. What was your favorite skit in this unit and why?
14. *Share a story:* Has anything embarrassing ever happened to you in public? Explain.
15. *Share a story:* Have you ever been tempted to laugh out loud in public at something, but you didn't to save somebody the embarrassment?

16. What should you do if you notice something, but it might embarrass someone if you pointed it out?
17. Why is it OK to tell good friends about potentially embarrassing situations they may be in?
18. Why is it not OK to tell strangers in general about potentially embarrassing situations they may be in?
19. Give an example of what you could ignore about an embarrassing situation you notice your teacher is in.
20. Give us an example of one embarrassing situation from a movie you have seen.
21. What is a good way to pretend not to notice something?
22. What do you want people to do for you if there is something potentially embarrassing about you, like a case of acne or a bad haircut?
23. *Time for a skit!* **Plot:** You come out of the bathroom with a friend, and you notice that she has toilet paper hanging out of her underwear. What do you say or do? The actors are you and a friend.
24. *Problem solving:* Richard has a problem. He gets confused about when he should make comments about potentially embarrassing situations in public and when he should just ignore what's going on and pretend not to notice. List three ways Richard could solve his problem, including one negative and two positive solutions.

SKILLS REVIEW

Instructor reads on Monday: Topics to review this week include:

1. Compliments
2. Personal Responsibility
3. Too Much Information
4. The Act of Pretending Not to Notice

Monday

The plan for the instructor: Host a "show and share" time. Students bring in artifacts or photographs to share with group members, who are seated on chairs in a circle. Each student has up to five minutes to talk about his or her interest while classmates ask questions. Play a board game if there is additional time.

Tuesday

The plan for the instructor: Instruct students to make posters of the review topics. Take photographs of students completing steps of the skills. Make sure each poster includes photographs, key words, and a written guide to the steps used to complete the skill. Display posters in the classroom or around school.

Wednesday

The plan for the instructor: Instruct students to finish their posters and share them with the class. Play a board game if there is additional time.

Thursday

The plan for the instructor: Show classroom videos of the skits. Also show a short video from the Internet—YouTube is often a good source—on one of the review topics: Compliments, Personal Responsibility, Too Much Information, and The Act of Pretending Not to Notice. The students are to watch the video and discuss what they liked about it and tips they learned.

Friday

The plan for the instructor: Play review bingo.

Bingo

Instructor reads: It's time for bingo. First I will read off a number and call on one of you to give an answer, make a comment, or demonstrate a skill. Everyone can cross off the numbers on the bingo sheets as they are called, and you win by getting five in a row.

1. Tell us the key points to keep in mind when giving a compliment.
2. Tell us the key points to keep in mind when receiving a compliment.
3. Tell us the key points to keep in mind when thinking of personal responsibility.
4. Tell us the key points to keep in mind so as to *not* share too much information.
5. What mistakes should you *avoid* when giving a compliment?
6. What mistakes should you *avoid* when receiving a compliment?
7. Give an example of someone taking personal responsibility for something.
8. What mistakes should you *avoid* when sharing personal information?
9. Give an example of two things you should avoid staring at in public?
10. Give an example of something OK to make comments about to your friend.
11. Demonstrate the *opposite* of taking personal responsibility for breaking a friend's iPad.

12. Demonstrate sharing too much information to acquaintances at dinner time about the last time you were sick. What *not* to do!
13. *Share your story:* Tell of a time when you took personal responsibility.
14. *Share your story:* Tell of a time when you ignored something potentially embarrassing in public.
15. Give a compliment to someone in this class.
16. *Share your story:* Tell of a time when you decided not to share too much information because you did not know the person you were talking to very well.
17. *Time for a skit!* With one other person, create a short skit. **Plot:** Practice taking personal responsibility at home with your mom after forgetting to take out the trash. First do it the wrong way, then the correct way. The actors are you and Mom.
18. *Time for a skit!* With another person, create a short skit on sharing too much information. **Plot:** You are tempted to tell someone you just met about all the problems you had in elementary school. First do it the wrong way, then the correct way. The actors are you and someone you just met.
19. *Time for a skit!* With another person, create a short skit on the act of pretending not to notice. **Plot:** You are with your dad and you see someone struggling to zip up his pants because the zipper is stuck. First respond the wrong way, then the correct way. The actors are you and Dad.
20. *Time for a skit!* With another person, create a short skit on responding to a compliment. **Plot:** A kid at school compliments you on your artistic talent. First respond the wrong way, then the correct way. The actors are you and a kid at school.
21. *Problem solving:* Teresa has a problem. Whenever she gives a compliment, it comes out sounding like an insult. Tell three ways Teresa could solve her problem, including one negative solution and two positive solutions.
22. *Problem solving:* Eric has a problem. He sees that an acquaintance's shirt is on inside out, but he doesn't know if he should tell him about it or not. Tell three ways he could solve his problem, including one negative solution and two positive solutions.

23. *Problem solving:* Leilani has a problem. Kids at school keep telling her how beautiful she is, and she doesn't know how to respond to their compliments. Tell three ways Leilani could deal with her problem, including one negative and two positive solutions.
24. Thinking back on the skills you learned in this unit, including compliments, personal responsibility, too much information, and the act of pretending not to notice, which was your favorite skill to learn about and why?

REFERENCES

Attwood, T. (2006). *The complete guide to Asperger's syndrome.* London, England: Jessica Kingsley Publishers.

Baron-Cohen, S. (2001). Theory of mind in normal development and autism. *Prisme, 34*, 174–183.

Bellini, S., Peters, J., Benner, L., & Hopf, A. (2007). A meta-analysis of school-based social skills interventions for children with autism spectrum disorder. *Journal of Remedial and Special Education, 28*(3), 153–162.

Buron, K. D., & Curtis, M. (2013). *The incredible 5-point scale: Assisting students with autism spectrum disorders in understanding social situations and in self-regulation.* Shawnee Mission, KS: AAPC.

Flavell, J. (2004). Theory of mind development: Retrospect and prospect. *Merrill Palmer Quarterly, 50*(3), 274–290.

Grandin, T. (2002). *Teaching ASD children and adults.* Retrieved from https://www.autism.com/advocacy_grandin_teaching

Gresham, F. M., Sugai, G., & Horner, R. H. (2001). Interpreting outcomes of social skills training for students with high-incidence disabilities. *Exceptional Children, 67*(3), 331–344.

Hattie, J., & Timperley, H. (2007). The power of feedback. *Review of Educational Research, 77*(1), 81–112.

Krasny, L., Williams, B. J., Provencal, S., & Ozonoff, S. (2003). Social skills interventions for the autism spectrum: Essential ingredients and a model curriculum. *Child and Adolescent Psychiatric Clinics of North America, 12*(1), 107–122.

Myles, B. S., Trautman, M. L., & Shelvan R. L. (2014). *The hidden curriculum: Practical solutions for understanding unstated rules in social situations.* Shawnee Mission, KS: AAPC.

Ramamoorthi, P., & Nelson, A. (2011). Drama education for individuals on the autism spectrum. In S. Schonmann (Ed.), *Key concepts in theatre/drama education* (177–181). Rotterdam, The Netherlands: Sense Publishers.

Rao, P., Beidel, D., & Murray, M. (2008). Social skills interventions for children with Asperger's syndrome or high functioning autism: A review and recommendations. *Journal of Autism and Developmental Disorders, 38*(2), 353–361.

Reichow, B., & Volkmar, F. (2010). Social skill interventions for individuals with autism: Evaluation for evidence-based practices within a best evidence synthesis framework. *Journal of Autism and Developmental Disorders, 40*, 149–166.

White, S., Oswald, D., Ollendick, T., & Scahill, L. (2009). Anxiety in children and adolescents with ASD. *Clinical Psychological Review, 29*(3), 216–229.

White, S. W., Keonig, K., & Scahill, L. (2007). Social skills development in children with autism spectrum disorders: A review of the intervention research. *Journal of Autism and Developmental Disorders, 37*(10), 1858–1868.

APPENDIX A

BINGO SHEETS

17	20	12	6	14
21	10	2	4	22
3	1	FREE	23	7
5	24	19	13	8
11	15	18	9	16

6	4	11	19	3
17	9	13	24	8
5	23	FREE	20	10
1	21	16	12	2
18	7	14	22	15

APPENDIX B

WARM-UP DISCUSSION TOPICS

1. What do you like to do in your free time?
2. What makes you happy?
3. What helps you most when you're sad?
4. What's your best part of the day at school?
5. Where were you born?
6. Who are your brothers and sisters?
7. What would you do with a million dollars?
8. What do you spend your money on?
9. Who in your family do you like to spend time with and why?
10. What is your favorite place in your house?
11. What's your favorite kind of candy?
12. What's your favorite fast food restaurant?
13. Have you ever had any jobs for pay?
14. What do you like to do on the Internet?
15. What kind of career would you like in the future?
16. Do you have any pets?
17. What are some of your favorite holiday shows?
18. What makes you laugh the most?
19. Where is one place you'd really like to go to on vacation?
20. Do you have any scars? If so, how did you get them?
21. What type of geographical terrain do you like?
22. What kind of movies do you like?
23. What kind of books do you like?
24. What are you afraid of?

25. What is one good birthday memory you've had?
26. If you could invite one famous person to your house, who would it be and what would you do?
27. If you could do a wonderful thing for the world, what would it be and why?
28. Have you ever been lost?
29. What kind of teacher do you like?
30. What's your favorite color?
31. What kind of clothes do you like to wear?
32. Are you sensitive to lights, noises, or the way something feels to you?
33. If you could change one thing about your life, what would it be and why?
34. Have you ever been bullied?
35. What kind of card or board games do you like to play?
36. What kind of TV shows do you like to watch?
37. Do you like to be surprised?
38. What's one thing that's really boring to you?
39. Where would you like to live in the future?
40. If you could have any pet you wanted, what would you get?
41. What are you thankful for?
42. What are some things you have that you would never sell?
43. What do you like to make with your hands?
44. What's a favorite present someone has given you?
45. If you could live forever, would you do it? Why or why not?
46. If you were president, what kind of laws would you make?
47. What do you like to do with your grandma or grandpa?
48. What kind of food do you like to make?
49. What bothers you about your classmates?
50. What do you like about your classmates?
51. What makes you worried?
52. How do you relax when you feel stressed?
53. If you could do anything you wanted for a day, what would you do?
54. Who do you admire and why?
55. When you are in a bad mood, what helps?
56. Would you rather ride a bike, ride a horse, or drive a scooter?
57. Can you play any instruments?

58. What do you like to sing?
59. What do you like to do on the weekends?
60. If you could eat only one meal for the rest of your life, what would it be?
61. Do you have any nicknames?
62. What sorts of things do you enjoy doing with other people?
63. What do you like to do in the summer?
64. What do you like to do in the winter?
65. What's your favorite season and why?
66. What's your favorite subject in school and why?
67. What three things do you plan to do after you graduate from high school?
68. Have you ever won any trophies or medals?
69. What are three words others might use to describe you?
70. What kinds of things do you like to do when you are alone?
71. Do you think it's ever OK to lie? Why or why not?
72. What funny movies or TV shows do you like?
73. If you could be anyone for a day, who would you be and why?
74. If you could have any game or toy you wanted, what would it be?
75. What do you like to do in nature?
76. What kind of exercise do you like?
77. If you could be born in another time, what time would choose and why?
78. If you could go to outer space, would you do it? Why or why not?
79. Who do you trust?
80. What kinds of things don't you like to touch?
81. What do you do when you need help with a problem?
82. What is your favorite part of the sky? Day or night sky? Explain.
83. What good advice do you try to listen to?
84. What's a happy memory for you?
85. What is one thing that your parents taught you that you really have tried to listen to?
86. If you had three wishes, how would you use them?
87. What do you like to do using technology?
88. What's the difference between a good friend and an acquaintance?
89. If you could change one thing about school, what would it be and why?
90. Do you think you can be trusted by others? Why or why not?
91. What smells do you like?

92. What kind of art do you like?
93. Which people in the community do you think have difficult jobs? Why?
94. What kind of vegetables do you like?
95. What kind of food grosses you out?
96. What is one thing most people don't know about you?
97. What is one thing you are good at doing?
98. Describe what you would do on a "perfect day."
99. What are your holiday traditions?
100. What is your proudest accomplishment?

CPSIA information can be obtained
at www.ICGtesting.com
Printed in the USA
LVHW100030040919
629871LV00004B/78/P

9 781942 197195